A CONTEMPORARY CONCEPT OF BOWING TECHNIQUE FOR THE DOUBLE BASS

By FREDERICK ZIMMERMANN

Table of Contents

ISBN 978-0-7935-1822-7

Visit Hal Leonard Online at
www.halleonard.com

PREFACE

Many of the technical problems presented in the playing of the double bass are problems peculiar to that instrument. They exist because of its physical structure and its manner of tuning.

The most formidable problems presented by the proportions of the double bass are the great distances separating notes and intervals, and the excessive number of shifts made necessary by the fact that only two semi-tones can be played in one position.

The solution to the problem of playing a complex, non-diatonic passage at a rapid tempo is sought in fingering as many notes (intervals), or orders of notes (chordal), as possible in one position. However, while this solves one problem, it creates another: it adds to the number of cross-string bowing changes.

An approach to the development of a technique relating to this particular problem is the subject of this work.

Fingerings function as guides, outlining generalizations and ''systems'', to train the fingers to move automatically in established and readily recognizable patterns.

The fingers trained to respond to

Example 1:

along the contours of the fingering pattern in

Example 2:

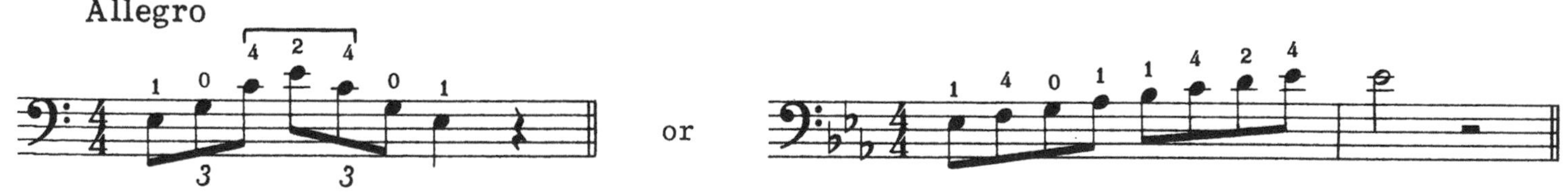

will do so as a reflex in whatever context this figure may occur (Mozart, Beethoven, Brahms, Storch-Hrabe, etc.).

Such a spontaneous recognition of and response to a figure does not, however, occur in the action of the bow arm. There are no precise guides, such as fingering indications, to clarify and make knowledgeable the nature and structure of the bowing patterns which seem to be, so to speak, woven in the very texture of the passage itself.

To abstract such bowing patterns from their particular environment or passage for ready indentification, classification, communication, detailed study and analysis is the main objective considered in organizing the material of this work.

Using measures from the last movement of the third Symphony of Beethoven, the method by which bowing patterns are abstracted is outlined as follows: The excerpt is written in the upper staff of a pair of bracketed staffs:

Example 3:

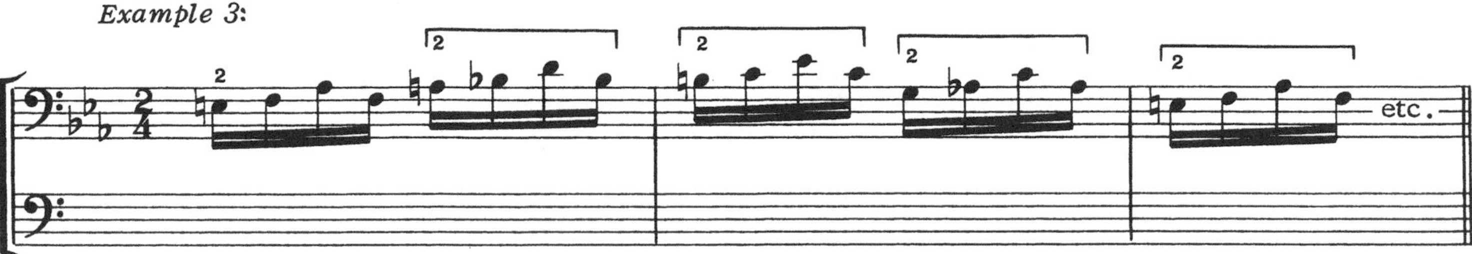

The pattern is written note for note on the lower staff as follows: Any note played on the "D" string is written on the lower staff, directly below that note as an "A" in the fourth position on the "D" string:

Example 3a:

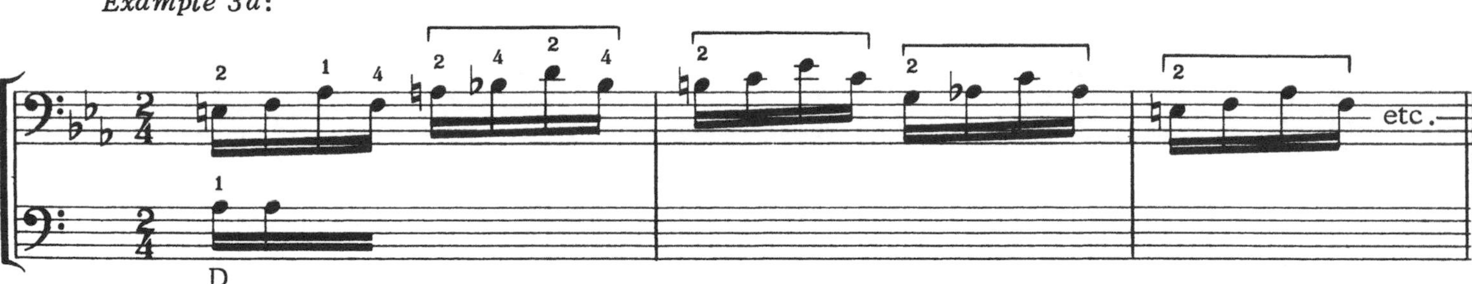

Any note played on the "G" string will be written on the lower staff, directly below that note as an "E" in the fourth position on the "G" string:

Example 3b:

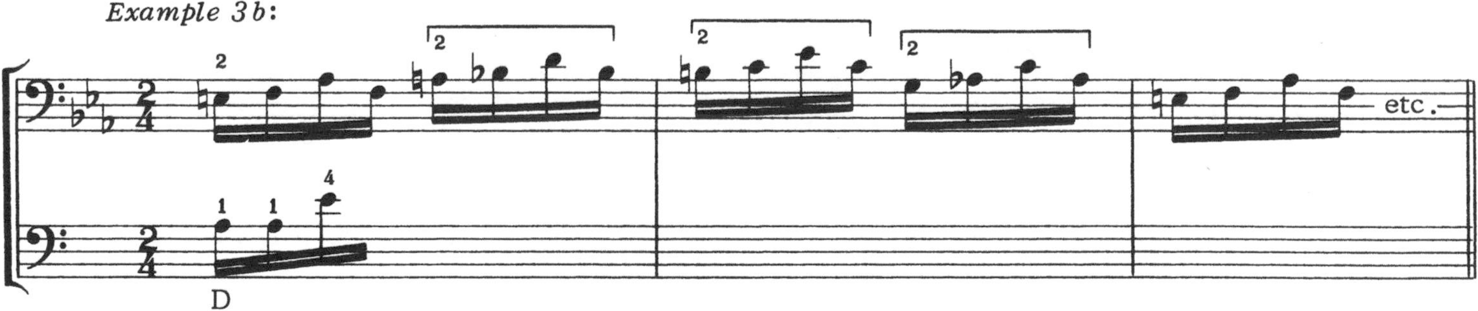

After carrying out the steps of this procedure throughout the excerpt, the bowing pattern will take the form or structure illustrated in

Example 3c:

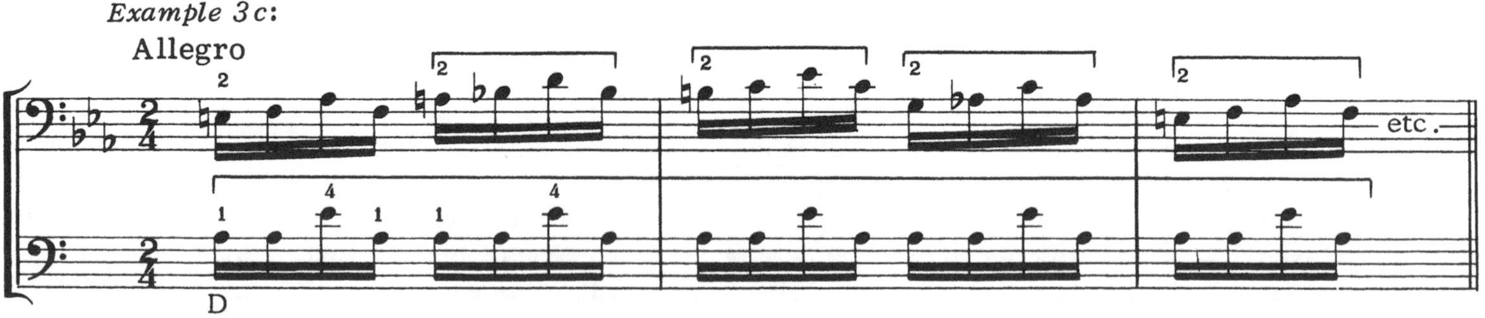

The bowing now has a visual arrangement, and it is interesting to note that though there are four shifts of position for the left hand, there is but one bowing pattern; an element of four notes repeated five times. This excerpt as well as any passage, can now be practiced in parts - the bowing first, free from the distracting movements of the left hand; then the left hand shifts can be practiced unhindered by any uncertain motions of the bow arm.

In passages across four strings, notes on the "A" string are written as an open "A"; those on the "E" string are written as an open "E".

One soon notices, in examining the patterns abstracted from the orchestral excerpts in this work, how often the basic elements of the various sections occur - either by themselves or in combination with one another. They are present throughout the entire literature, regardless of the key, style or form of a composition.

The basic elements of each section, such as those of Section 1, and their inversions

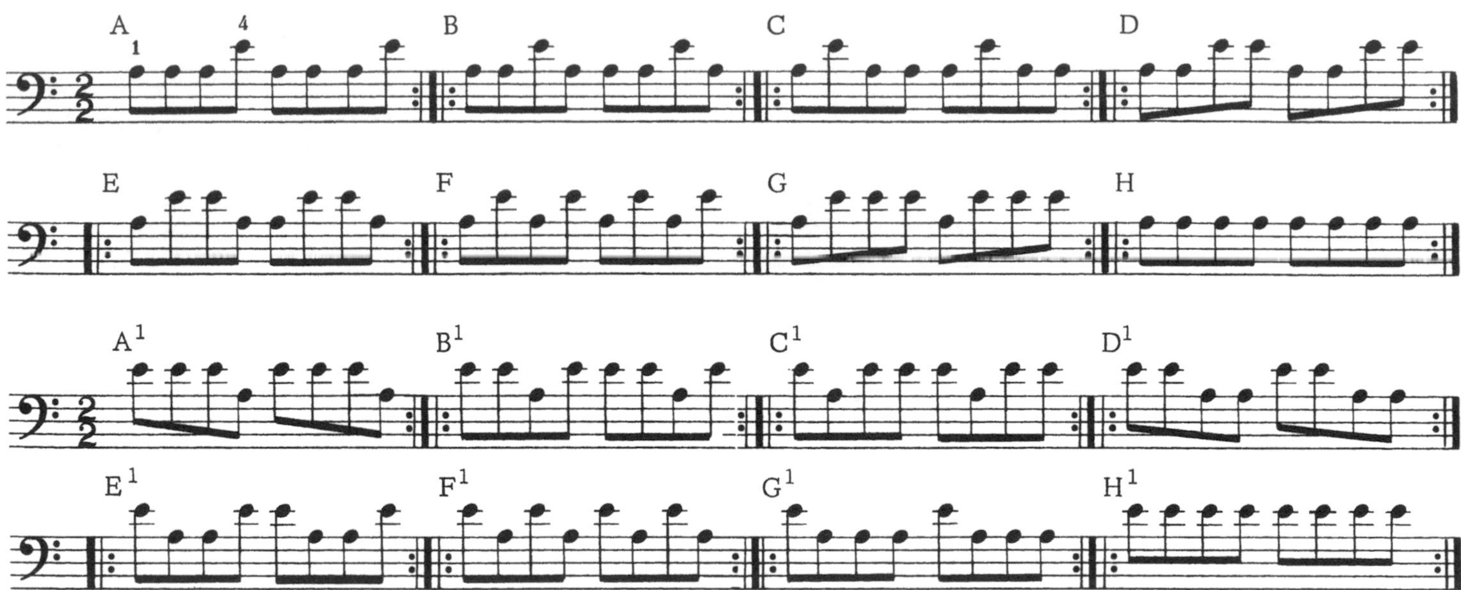

should be studied together with the visual guide (graph) of each in detail, before going on to the next, since the understanding and skill with which one pattern is played (repeatedly) depends on the knowledge and assurance one has gained from the previous pattern, though each separate one is a new experience in controlling the alternating movements of the bow.

The general format of this work includes a preface (the object and purpose of this work); an introduction (description of the functions of the arm and hand, and the purpose of their functions and supplementary material), and six sections.

Sections 1 to IV are subdivided into these parts:

1. The Basic Patterns.
2. Suggested Practice Procedure.
3. Etudes constructed on the Basic Patterns and Permutations of Their Elements.
4. Bowings and Etudes Built on the Bowing Patterns.
5. Examples from Etudes, Orchestral Passages and Materials from the Solo Repertoire.
6. Graphic Bowing Charts.

Section V:

Patterns, Etudes and Excerpts Relating to Three and Four Strings.

Section VI:

Bowing Drills.

There are over four hundred bowing patterns forming the main portion of this book. Though not an attempt to exhaust all the possibilities, they serve as a sufficient basis for further study, reference, serious consideration and expansion. Their efficacy will be realized in proportion to the manner in which they are used. To have a knowledge of some is to bring a technique to the solution of a bowing problem; to have command of many is to face the materials of music with confidence and skill.

- - Frederick Zimmermann

INTRODUCTION

There are two considerations which are of major importance in the course of practicing cross-string bowing patterns. First, the hair of the bow must remain as close to the strings as possible, in the particular pattern being studied; and second, the raising and lowering movements of the arm must be kept at a minimum.

The technique of bowing across two or more strings is a total operation consisting of three principal parts, each part acting in accord with the others:

1. The horizontal movements of the bow arm.
2. The raising and lowering motions of the arm.
3. The tilting actions of the hand.
    a. A sub-phase is the feeling of the weight of the arm. This sensation of weight (the actual weight of the arm) is carried along the intricate motions of all the cross-string patterns.

Each stage in turn has its specific function and purpose:

1. The horizontal movements of the arm direct the bow in either alternate or successive down and up-bow motions. They also serve to regulate the various rates of speed (velocity) at which the bow travels.
2. The raising and lowering motions of the arm tilt or direct the bow to either a lower or a higher pitched string.
3. The tilting action of the hand turns the stick of the bow toward the fingerboard in going to a higher pitched string, and away from it in going to a lower pitched string. This motion is auxiliary to and coincidental with the gradual raising and lowering movements of the arm, and serves to reduce its movements considerably. Both actions operate in accord, thus effecting smooth and facile string crossing.

The following exercises are included as outlines intended to train the hand and arm to move with an economy of motion from one string surface to another. The tilting action of the hand is valid for both styles of bowing, except that when using the *French Bow* there is more wrist movement, whereas when using the *Dragonetti Bow* (German) there is oblique wrist and forearm motion.

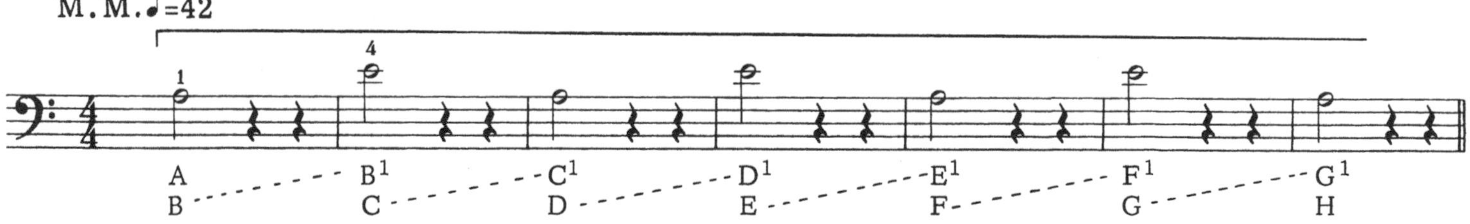

1. Stroke the note "A"; pause after the full durational value has been realized. (A to B)

Diagram 1:

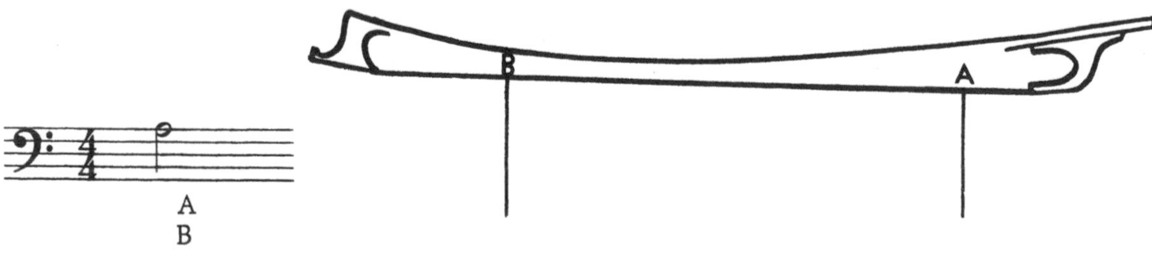

2. During the period of rest tilt the bow slowly, in the direction of the fingerboard, until the hair of the bow finds the surface of the "G" string, engaging it securely preparatory to stroking the note "E". (see Diagram 2.) (B to B^1)

Diagram 2:

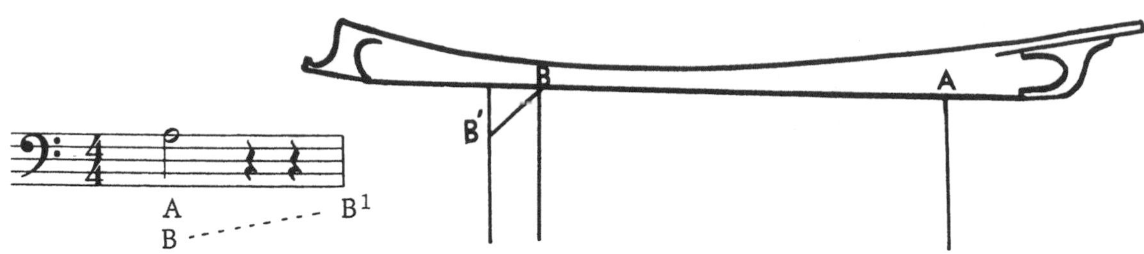

3. Stroke the note "E"; pause after the durational value has been realized. (see Diagram 3.) (B^1 to C)

Diagram 3:

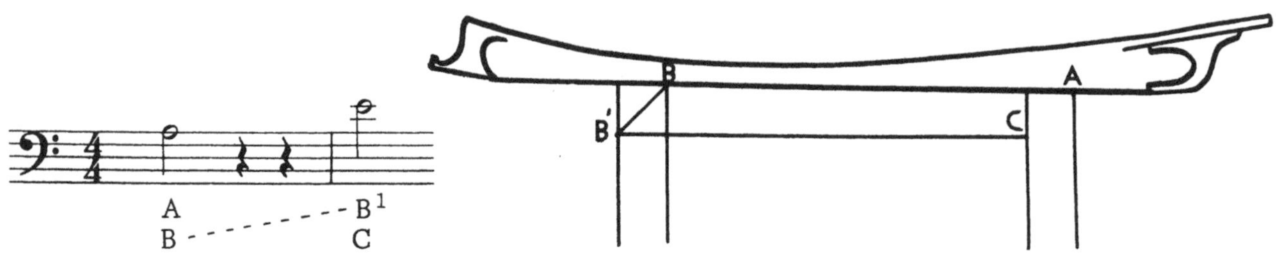

4. During the period of rest, tilt the bow slowly, away from the fingerboard, until the hair of the bow finds the surface of the "D" string, engaging it securely, preparatory to stroking the note "A". (C to C^1)

Diagram 4:

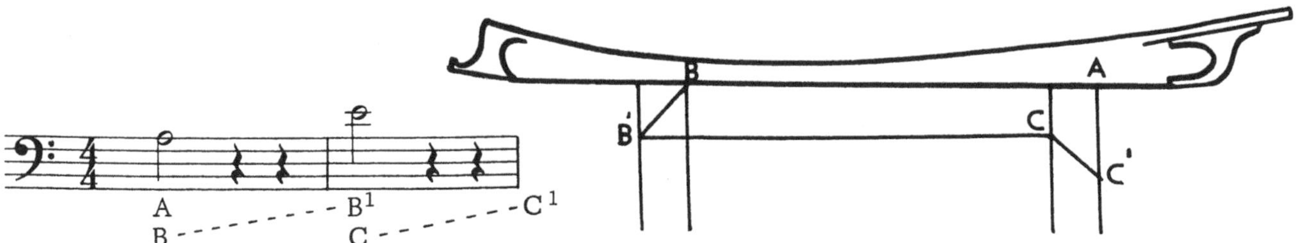

5. Stroke the "A"; pause after the durational value has been realized.

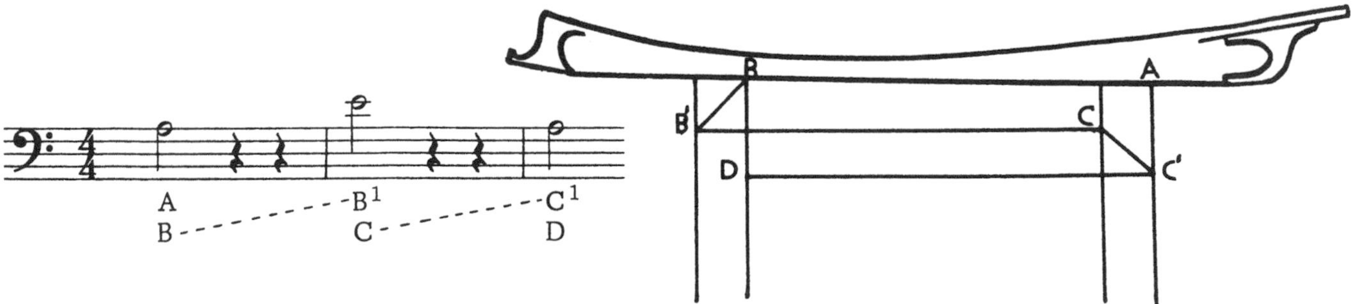

6. Repeat the steps as outlined in phases 1 to 4 (C to D, D^1 to E, E^1 to F, F^1 to G, G^1 to H).

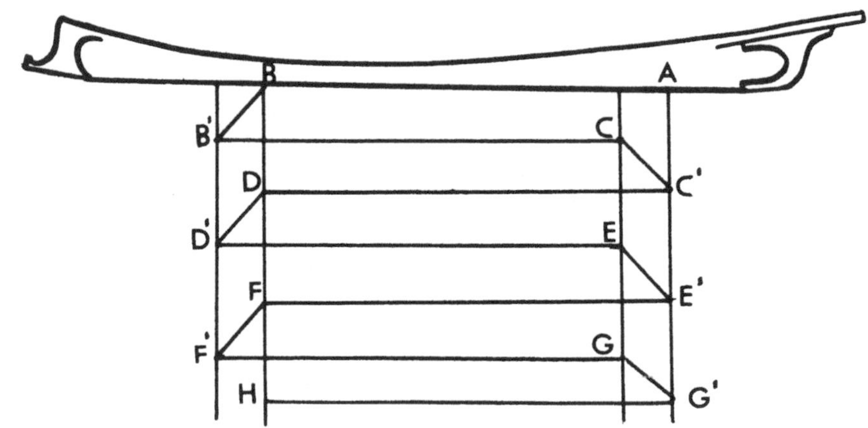

1. During the stroking of the first half of measure 1 (the sounding of the "A"), gradually tilt the bow toward the surface of the "G" string, as close as possible, without actually resonating it. Gauge the speed of the bow and its distance from the "G" string.

2. On the count of three, gently and delicately move the bow across the "G" string without any acceleration of speed or change in dynamics, thereby sounding and sustaining the double-stop for the remainder of the measure.

3. Raise the bow but slightly from the surface of the "D" string while sounding the "E" again.

4. While stroking the "E", gradually tilt the bow toward the surface of the "D" string, as close as possible, without actually resonating it. Gauge the speed (velocity) of the bow and its distance from the "D" string, preparatory to sounding the note "A", then repeat phases 1 to 4.

♩ = 72

♩ = 72

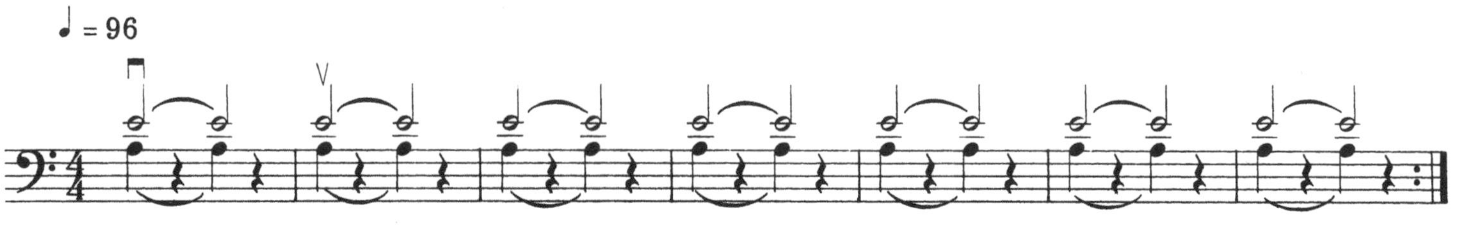
♩ = 96

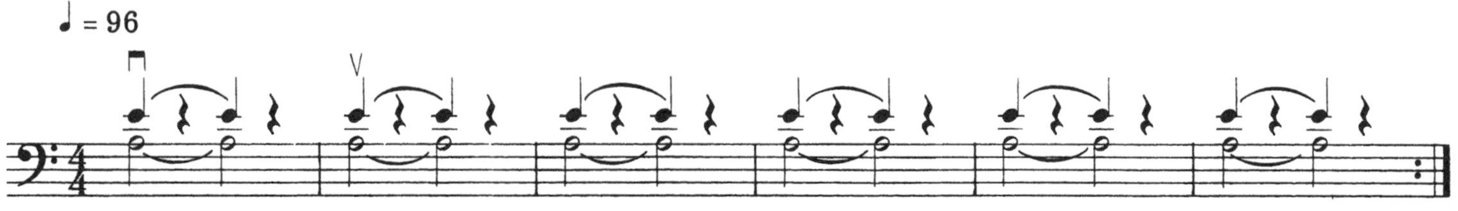
♩ = 96

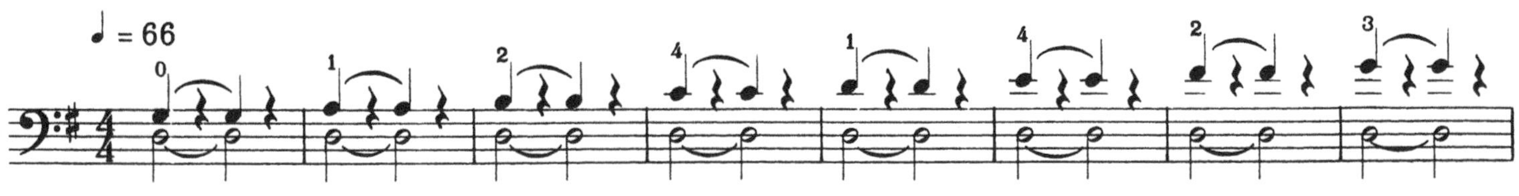
♩ = 66
0
1
2
4
1
4
2
3

3
2
4
1
4
2
1
0

♩ = 69
♩ = 72
♩ = 72
mf
♩ = 72
mf

It is also important to the overall objective of developing a fine bowing technique, that the metric and durational values be kept under control. Since the rhythmic and metric beats in these examples and exercises are one and the same, care must be taken to accent only the primary and secondary beats, to avoid any alteration, in pattern or meter, caused by the accidental emphasis placed on a note by the mere act of crossing the string, as illustrated in the following figures.

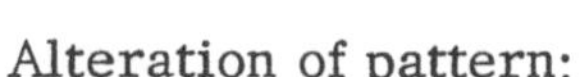
Alteration of pattern:

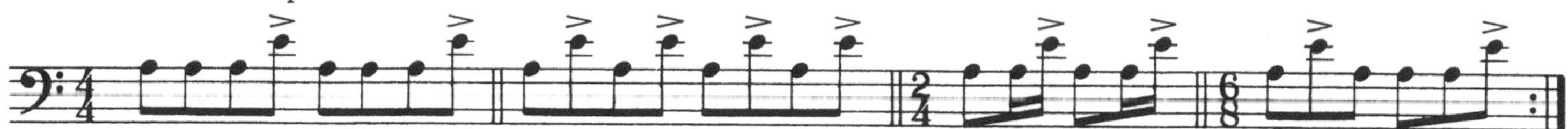

Alteration of meter:

Alteration of durational values:

A compound of faults:

There are numerous instances, however, when non-metric beats are accented, as in the following excerpt, from the overture to *Der Freischütz*, by Carl Maria von Weber, in which the composer indicates a stronger emphasis on the last beats of the first four measures, and on the second and fourth beats of the following measures:

The metronome markings, suggested by the writer, are to be used for the practice of the various abstracted patterns throughout the sections of this book. It is advisable also to practice them one notch above as well as one notch below the metronome marks indicated.

SECTION I

PATTERN I

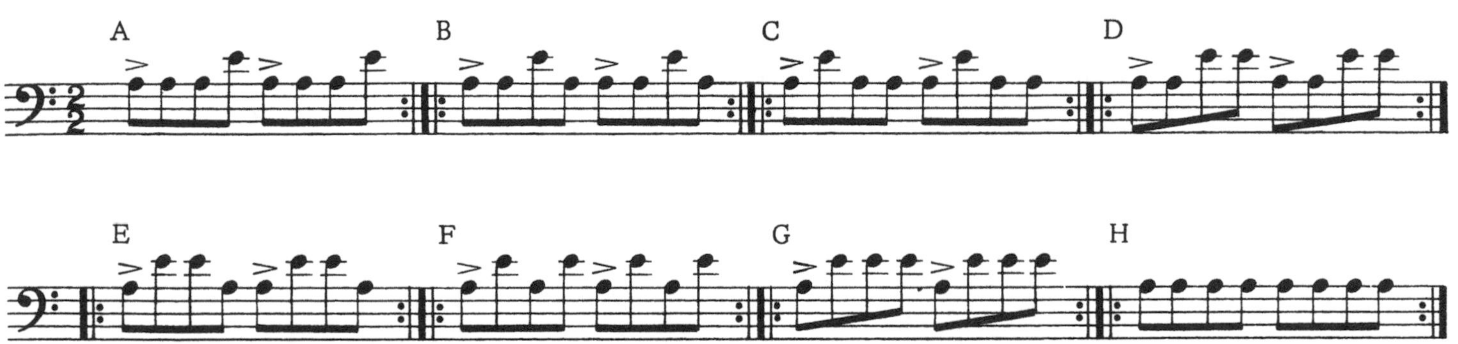

SUGGESTED PROCEDURE FOR PRACTICE

Begin each measure with the metronome set at 𝅗𝅥 = 72 (two beats to a measure). These are to be played with a détaché bowing; a smoothly articulated stroke with no pause or break between the notes. When the movements of the arm and hand feel comfortable and the crossing motion secure and well directed, advance the mark to 𝅗𝅥 = 88. Again, when these are played with a feeling of ease and control, advance to 𝅗𝅥 = 104. Play each measure keeping the metronome at 𝅗𝅥 = 104, using a spiccato bowing. When these are played with a sense of ease and control, increase the metronome marking step-wise to 𝅗𝅥 = 116 and 𝅗𝅥 = 126. At an advanced marking of 𝅗𝅥 = 132 to 𝅗𝅥 = 152, the bow is again moved with a rapid détaché bowing.

ETUDE

PATTERN I

♩ = 92 *(spiccato)*, ♩ = 126 *(détaché)*

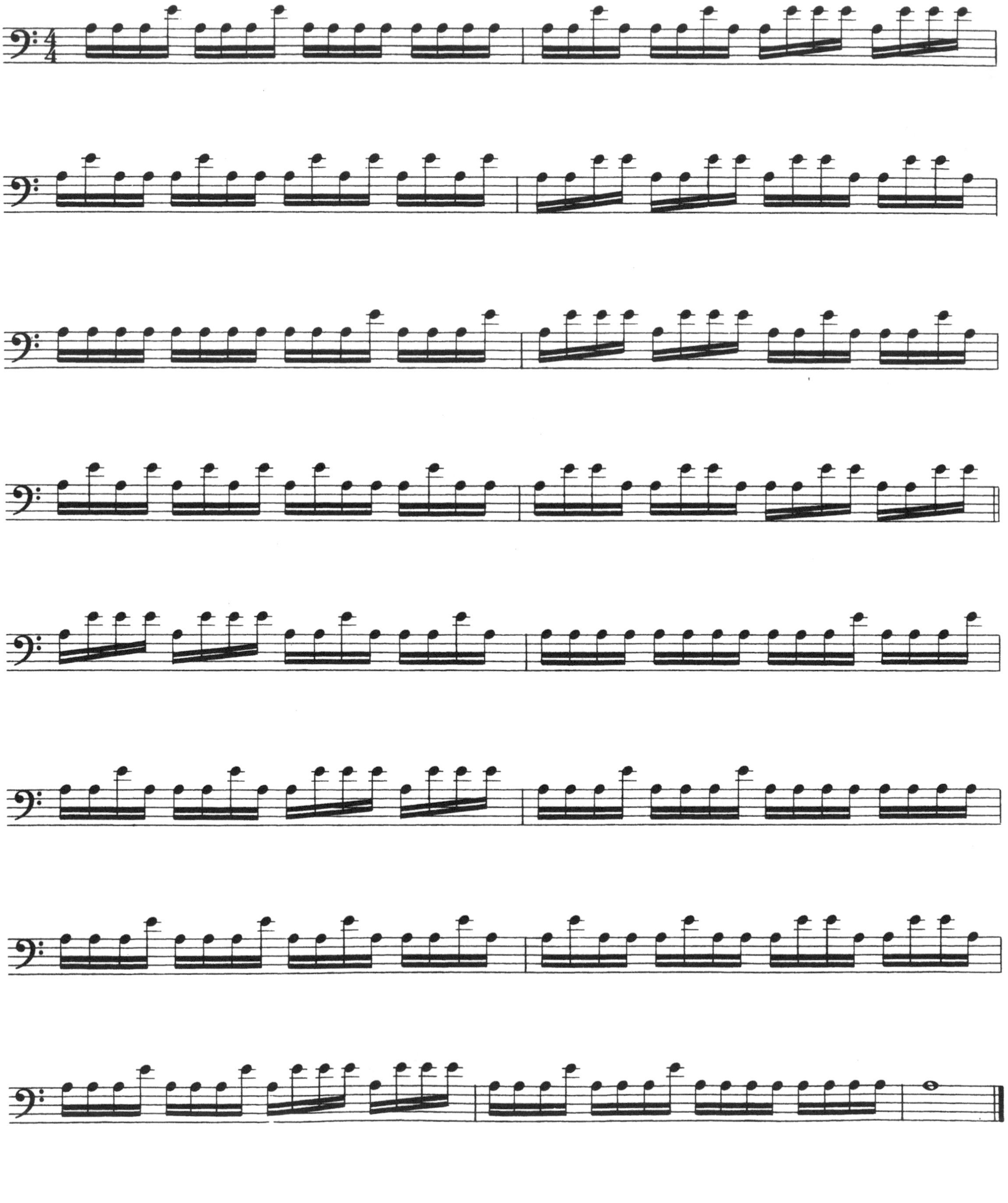

PERMUTATIONS OF PATTERN I

E A E B E C
E D E F E G E H
F A F B F C
F D F E F G F H
G A G B G C
G D G E G F G H
H A H B H C
H D H E H F H G

ETUDES

PERMUTATIONS OF PATTERN I

Allegro ♩ = 96 *(spiccato)*

Allegro molto ♩ = 112 *(spiccato)*

BOWINGS

PATTERN I

* The dotted notes are to be played alternately on the string *(Staccato)* and off the string *(Flying Spiccato)*.

ETUDE

BOWINGS (PATTERN I)

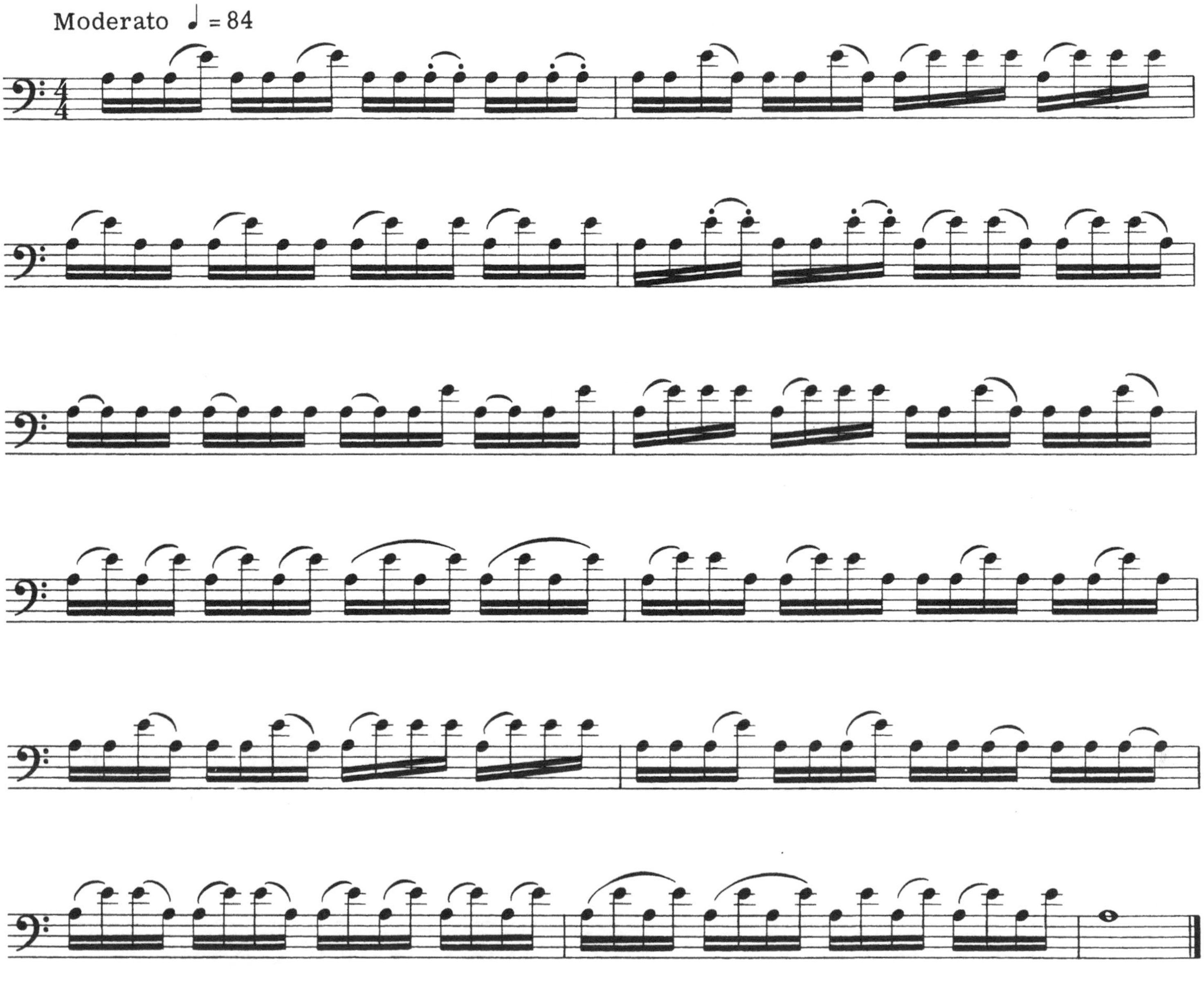

Moderato ♩ = 84

PATTERN II

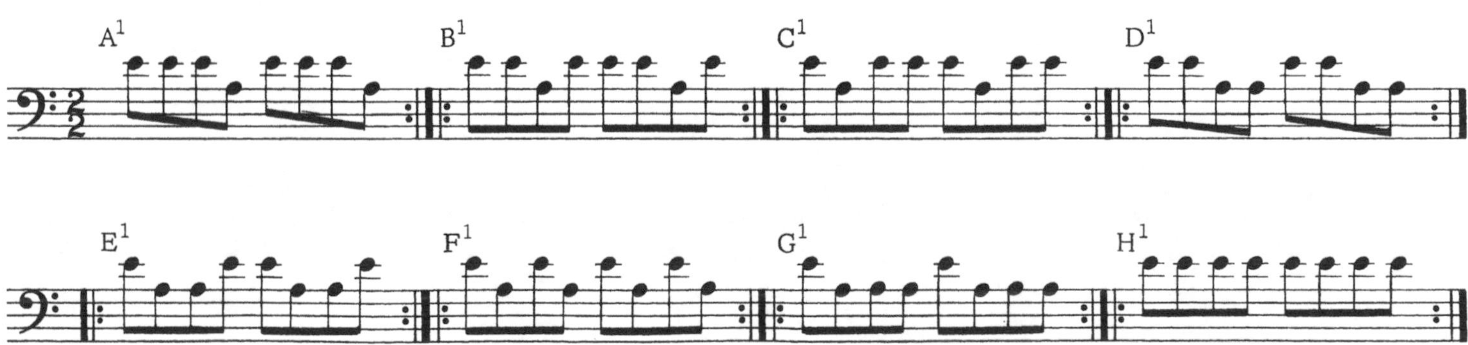

PERMUTATIONS OF PATTERN II

E1
A1
E1
B1
E1
C1
E1
D1
E1
F1
E1
G1
E1
H1
F1
A1
F1
B1
F1
C1
F1
D1
F1
E1
F1
G1
F1
H1
G1
A1
G1
B1
G1
C1
G1
D1
G1
E1
G1
F1
G1
H1
H1
A1
H1
B1
H1
C1
H1
D1
H1
E1
H1
F1
H1
G1

ETUDE

PATTERN II

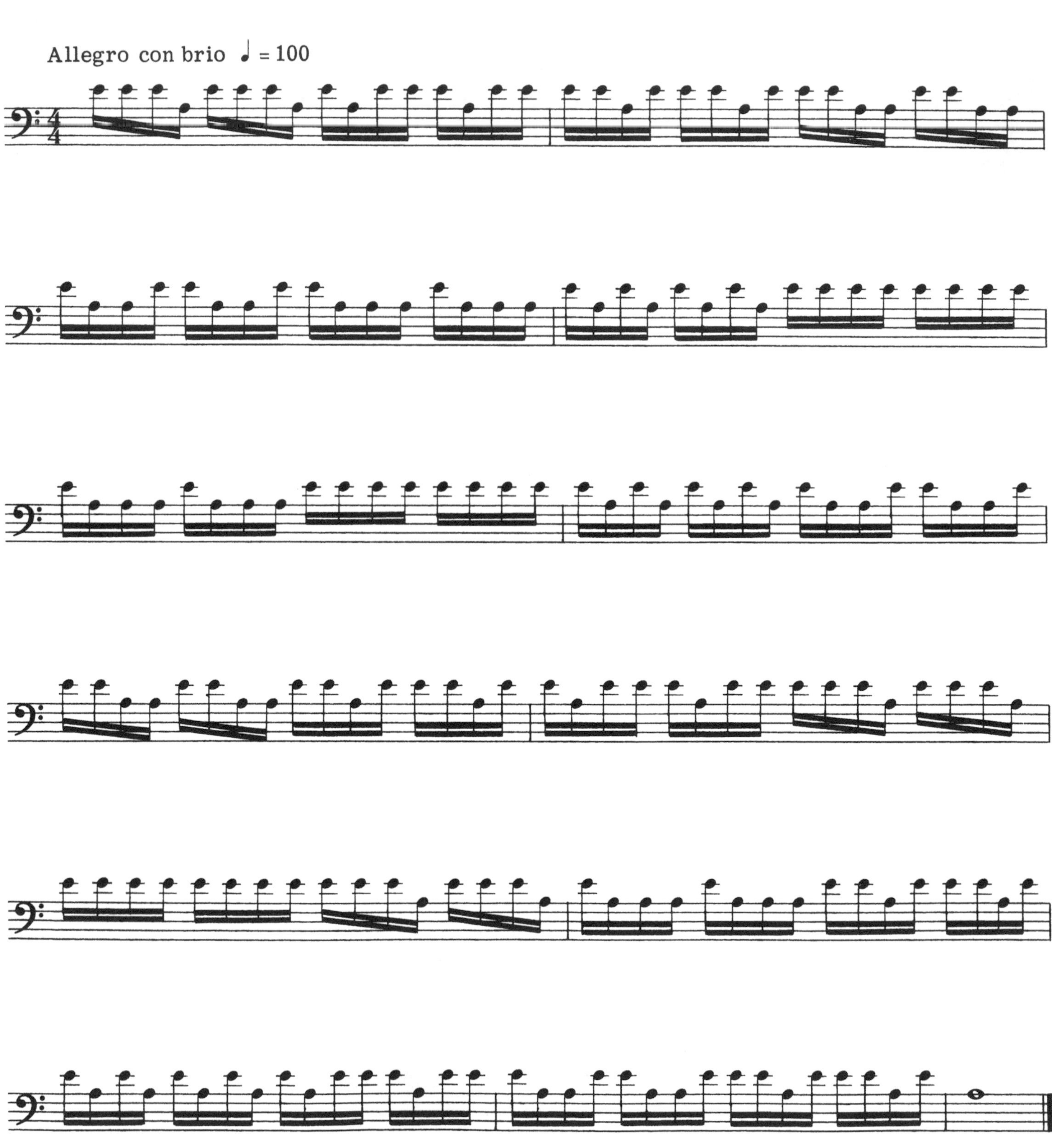

ETUDES

PERMUTATIONS OF PATTERN II

Allegro non troppo ♩ = 88

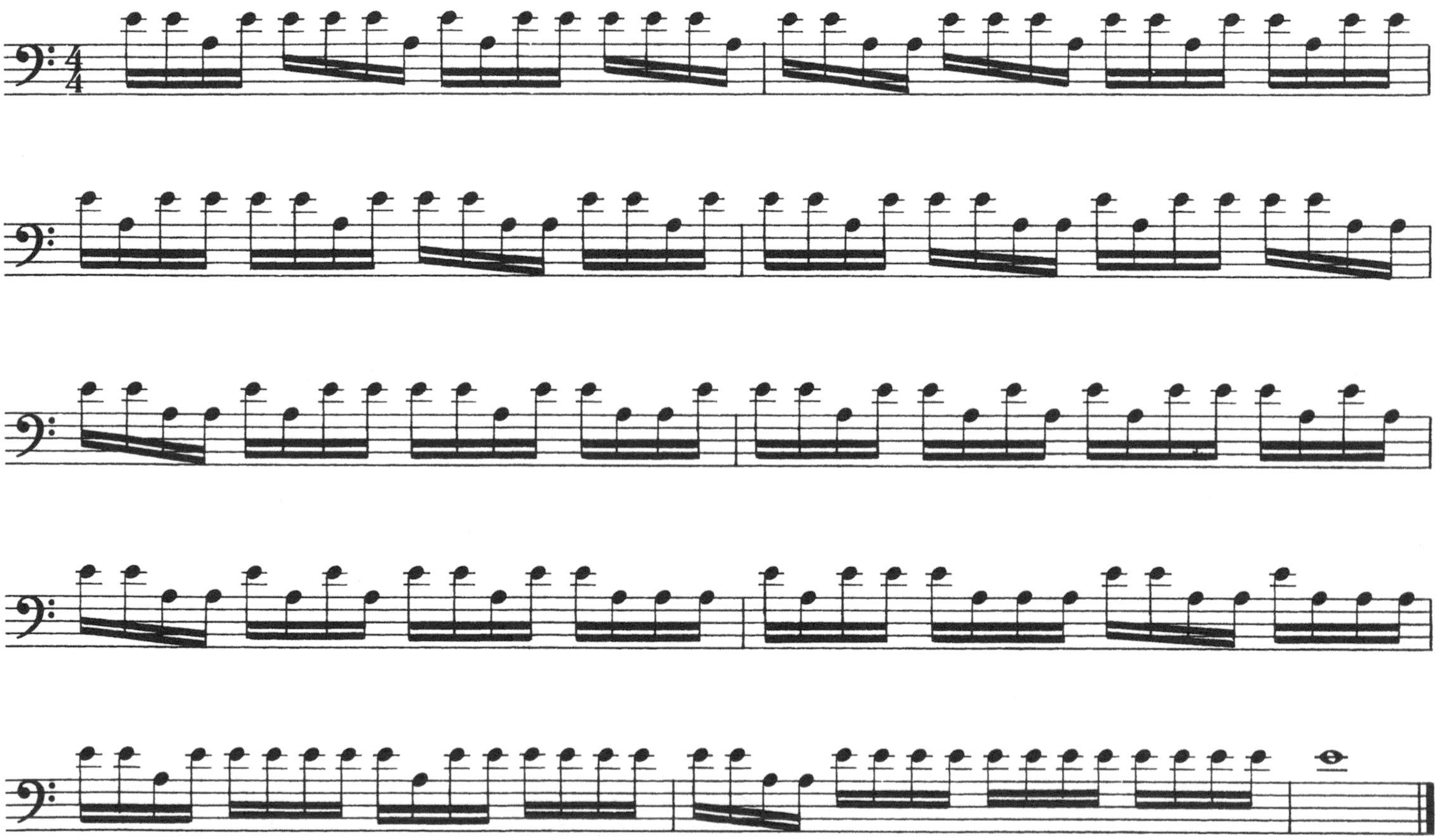

Allegro ♩ = 92

BOWINGS

PATTERN II

*The dotted notes are to be played alternately on the string *(Staccato)* and off the string *(Flying Spiccato)*.

ETUDE

BOWINGS (PATTERN II)

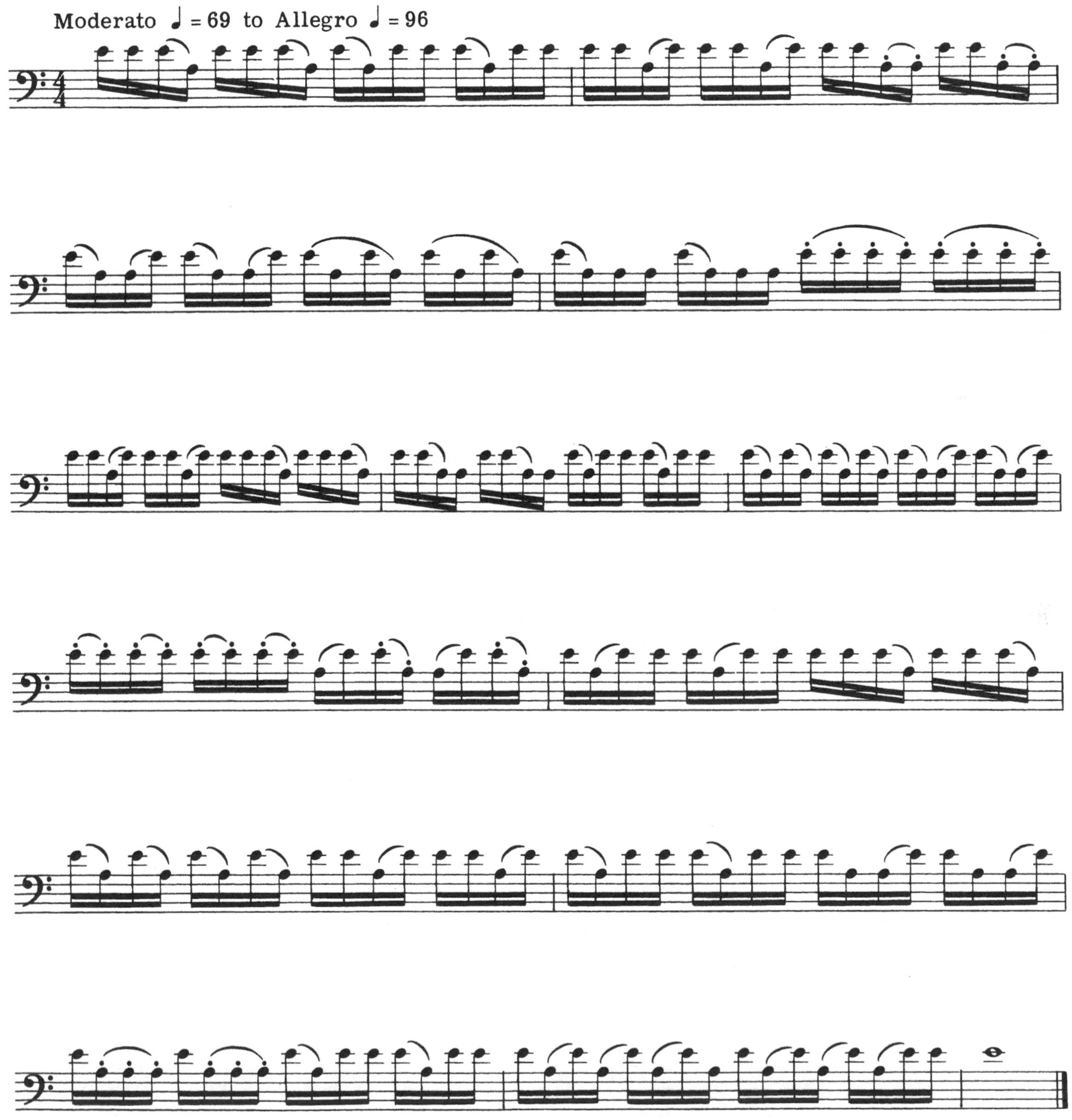

PERMUTATIONS OF PATTERNS I & II

E A1 E B1 E C1 E D1
E E1 E F1 E G1 E H1
F A1 F B1 F C1 F D1
F E1 F F1 F G1 F H1
G A1 G B1 G C1 G D1
G E1 G F1 G G1 G H1
H A1 H B1 H C1 H D1
H E1 H F1 H G1 H H1

ETUDES

PEMUTATIONS OF PATTERNS I & II

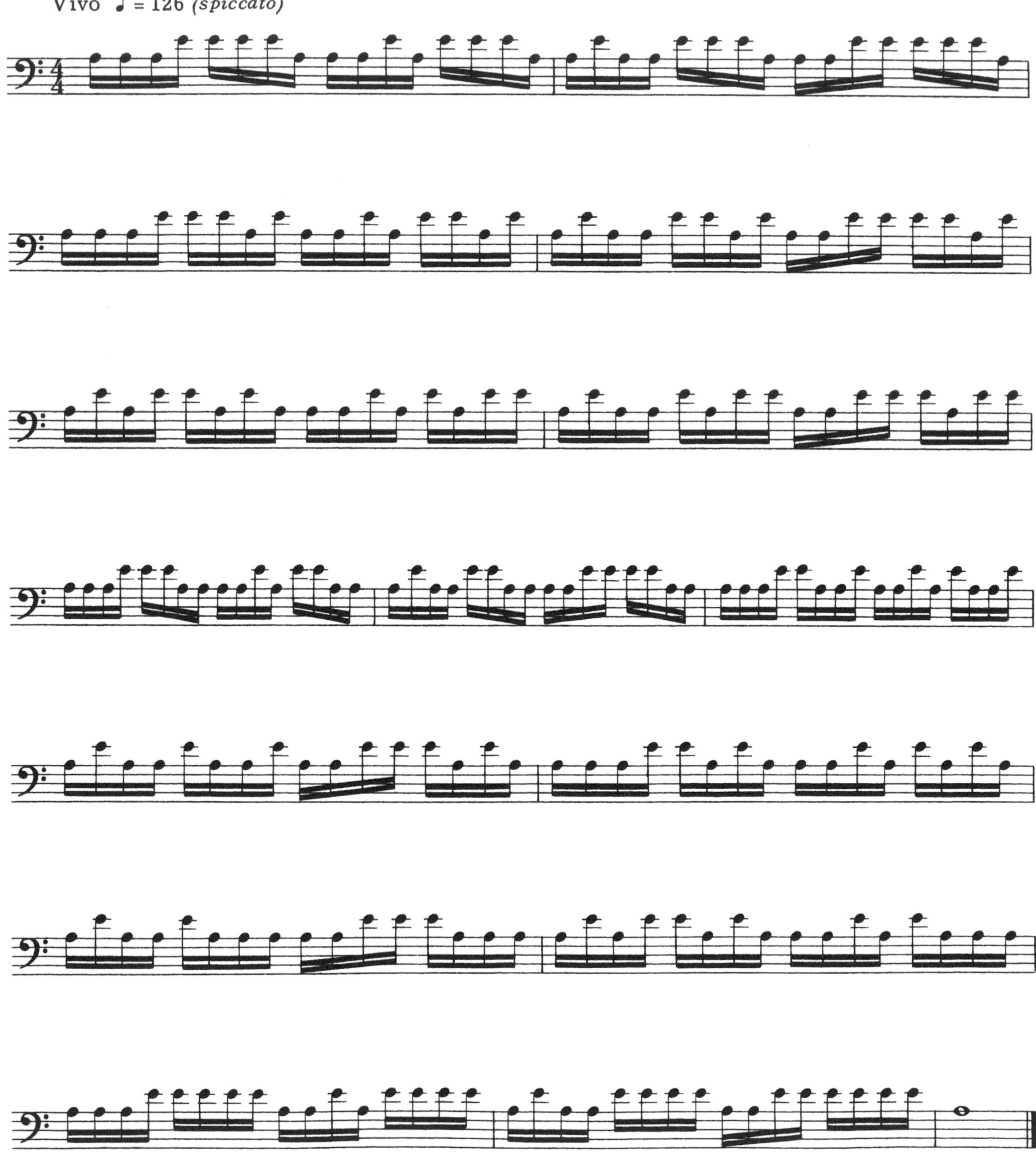

This exercise is to be practiced with a Martelé bowing; each note beginning with a sharp attack and separated from the next note.

Allegro giusto ♩ = 100

ETUDES

BOWINGS (PATTERNS I & II)

Allegro non troppo ♩= 88

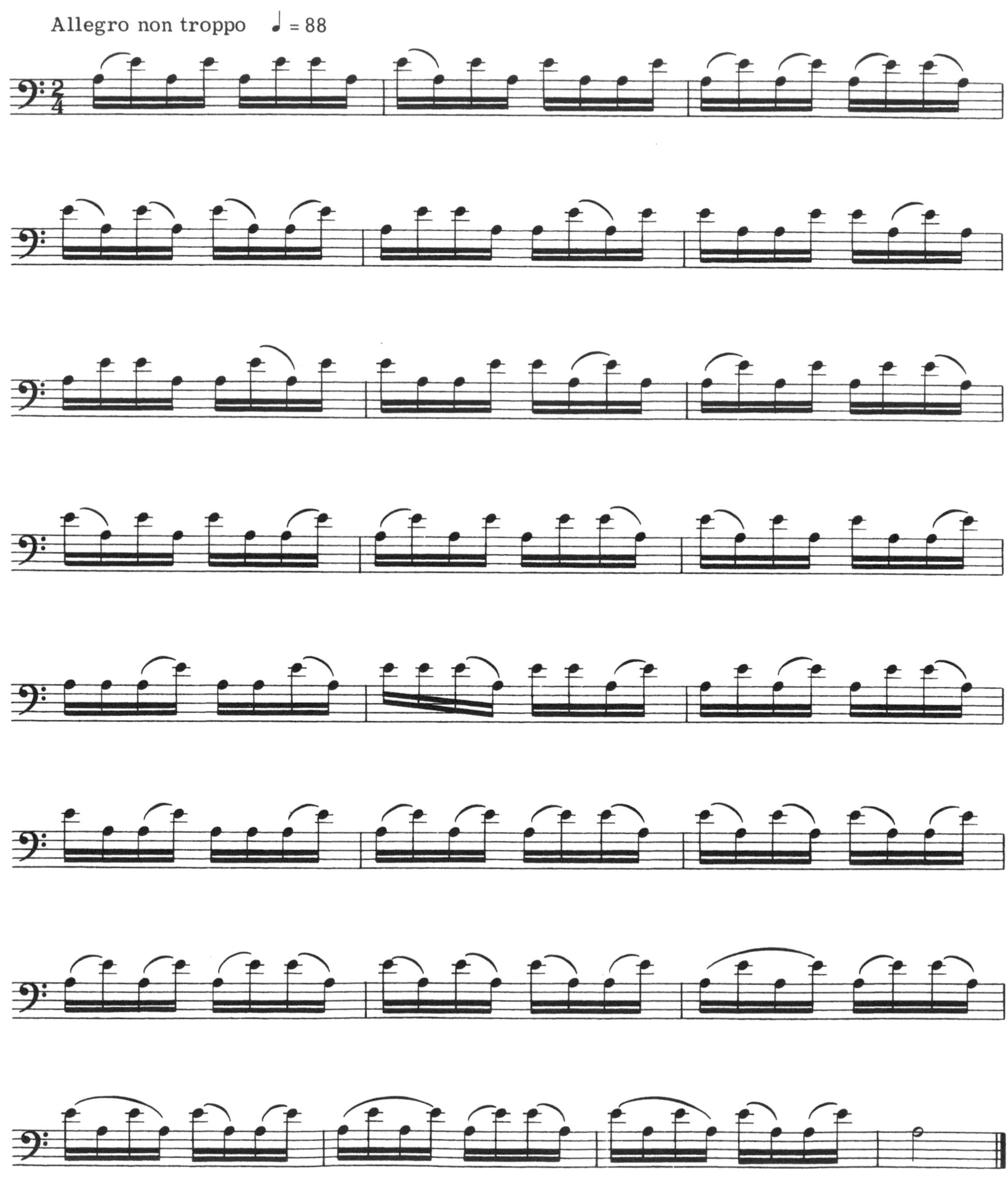

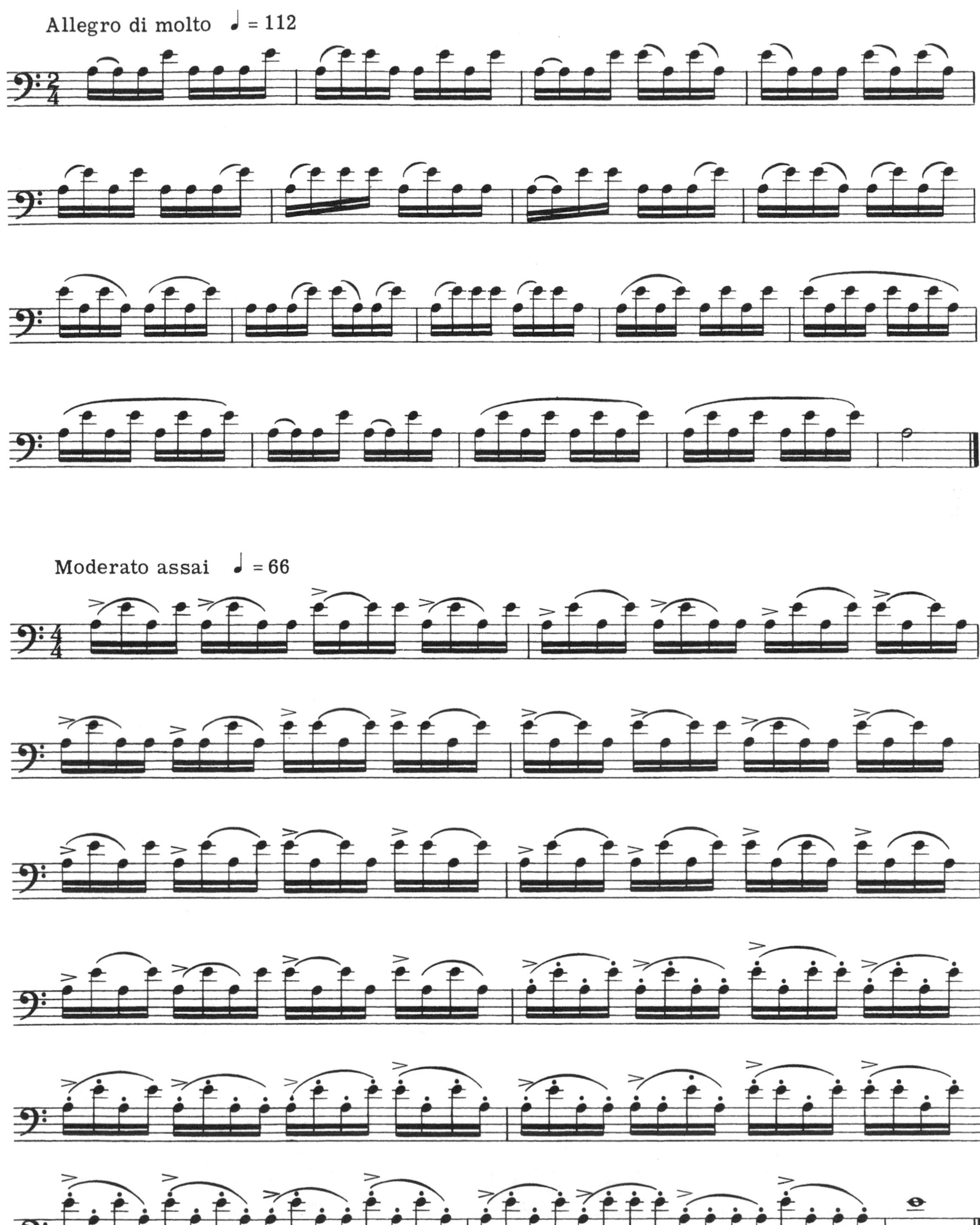
Allegro di molto ♩ = 112
Moderato assai ♩ = 66

(PERMUTATIONS OF PATTERNS I & II

E1
A
E1
B
E1
C
E1
D
E1
E
E1
F
E1
G
E1
H
F1
A
F1
B
F1
C
F1
D
F1
E
F1
F
F1
G
F1
H
G1
A
G1
B
G1
C
G1
D
G1
E
G1
F
G1
G
G1
H
H1
A
H1
B
H1
C
H1
D
H1
E
H1
F
H1
G
H1
H

ETUDES

PERMUTATIONS OF PATTERNS II & I

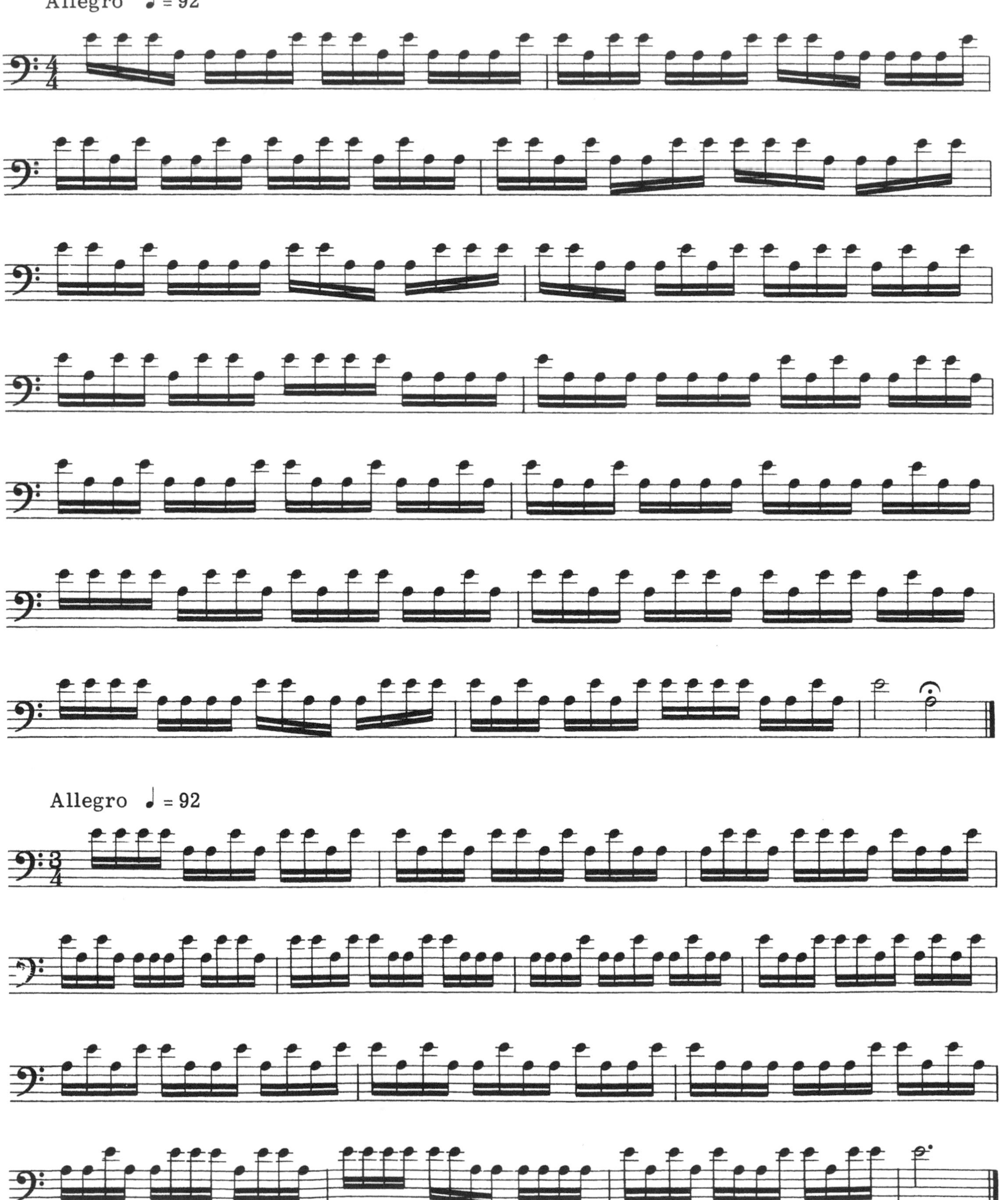

ETUDES

BOWINGS (PERMUTATIONS OF PATTERNS II & I)

Allegro assai ♩ = 100

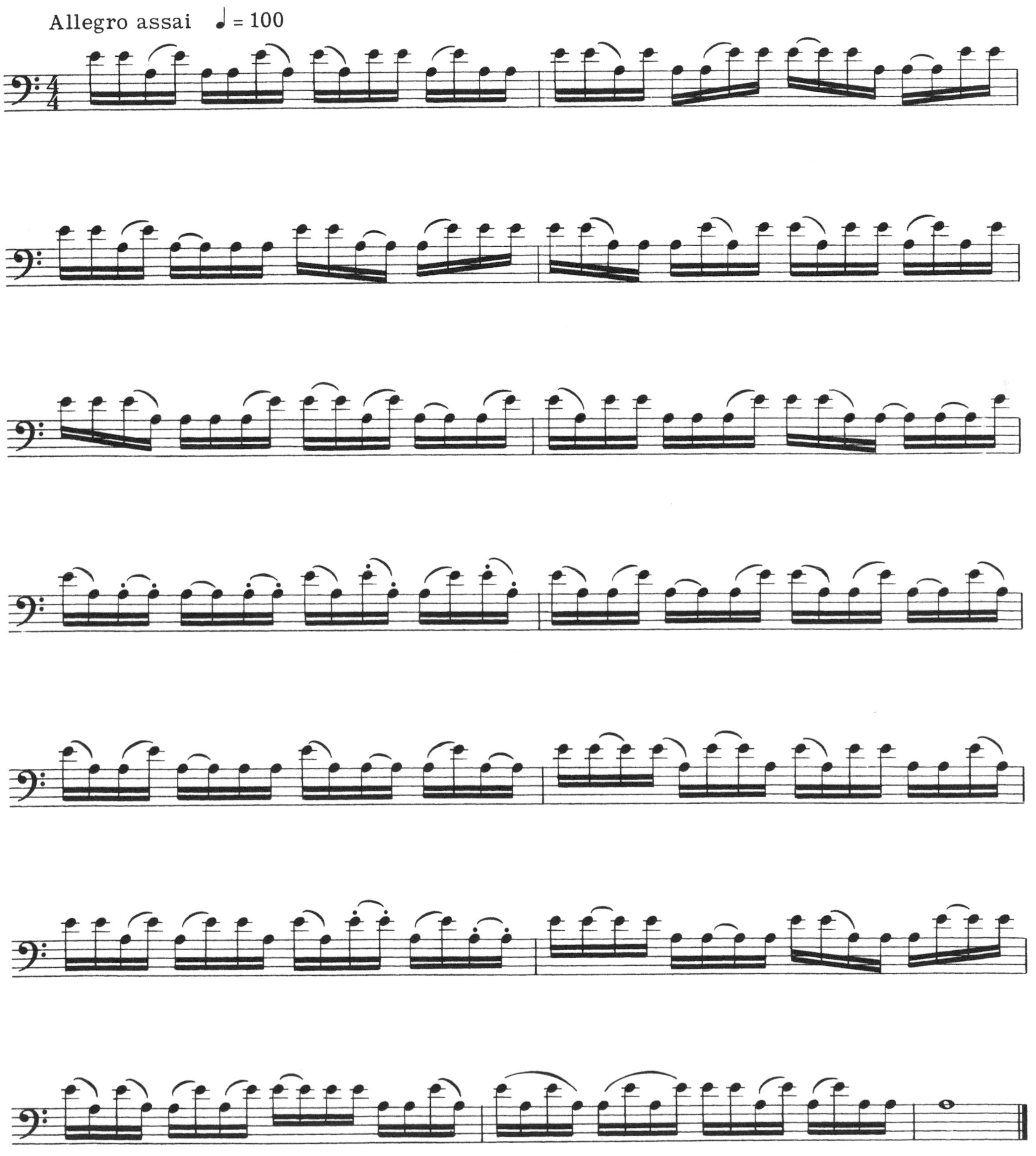

SYMPHONY No. 40

WOLFGANG A. MOZART

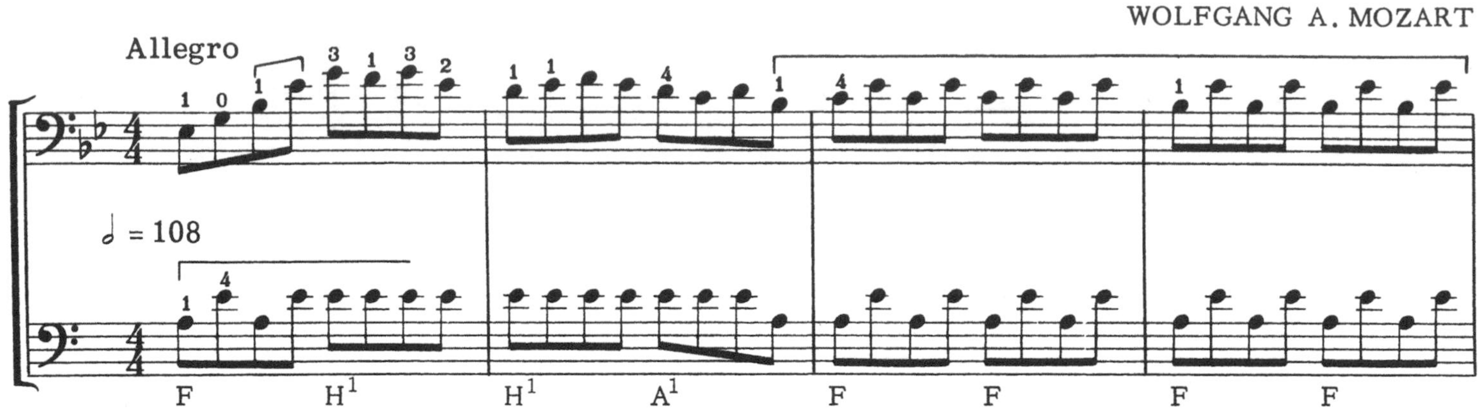

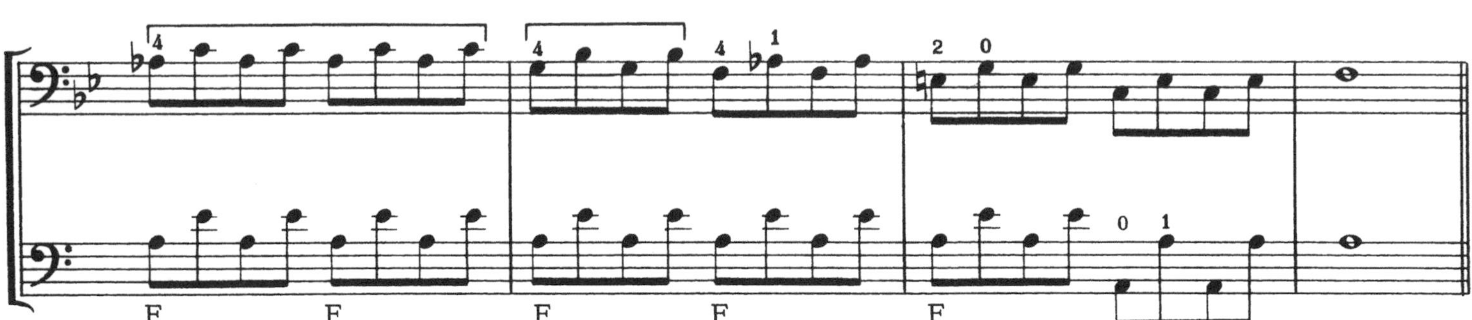

Combined in the first measure of this example are F of pattern I and H[1] of pattern II, one of the many permutations of patterns I and II.

In measure two we find H[1] and A[1] permutations of the basic patterns. Measures three, four, five and six are repetitions of the basic pattern F. Measure seven consists of an element of F and an alternate crossing between the D and the A strings.

Subsequent examples will be similarly notated, using symbols corresponding with each section.

PIANO CONCERTO No. 4

LUDWIG VAN BEETHOVEN

Vivace

♩ = 108

G G H A C¹ C¹ C¹ H¹

SYMPHONY No. 34

WOLFGANG A. MOZART

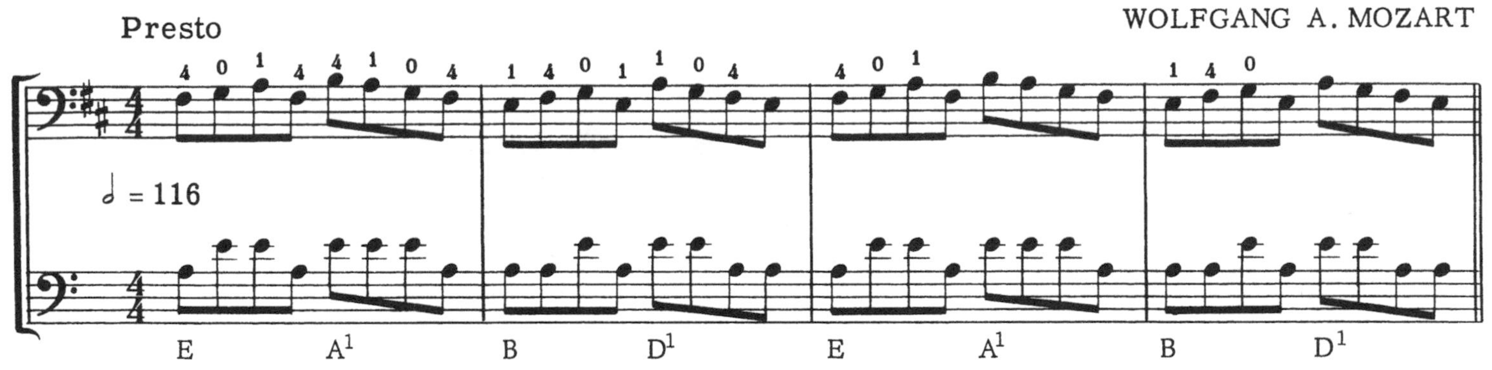

CONCERTO

DOMENICO DRAGONETTI

CONCERTO

E. D. STEIN

ETUDE

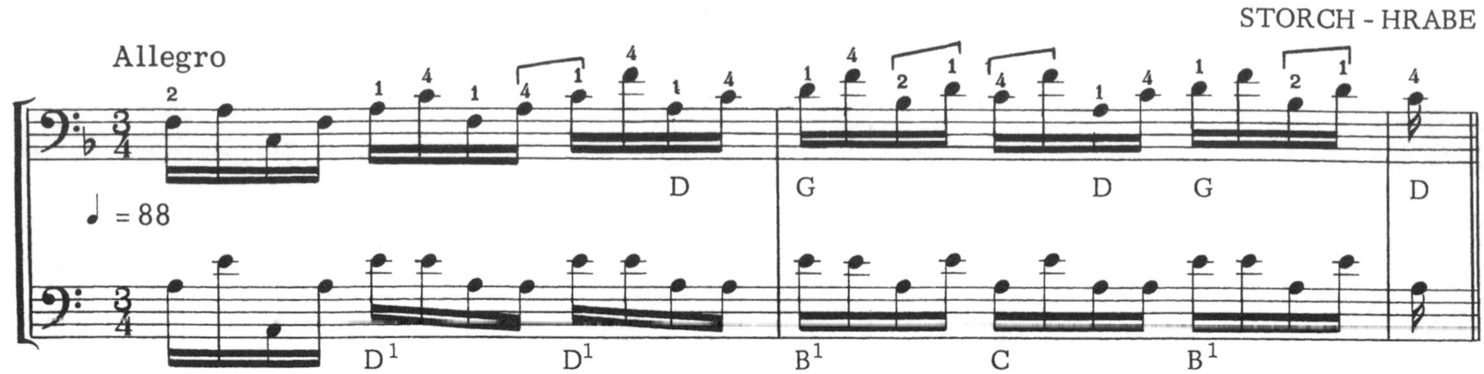

CONCERTO

ETUDE

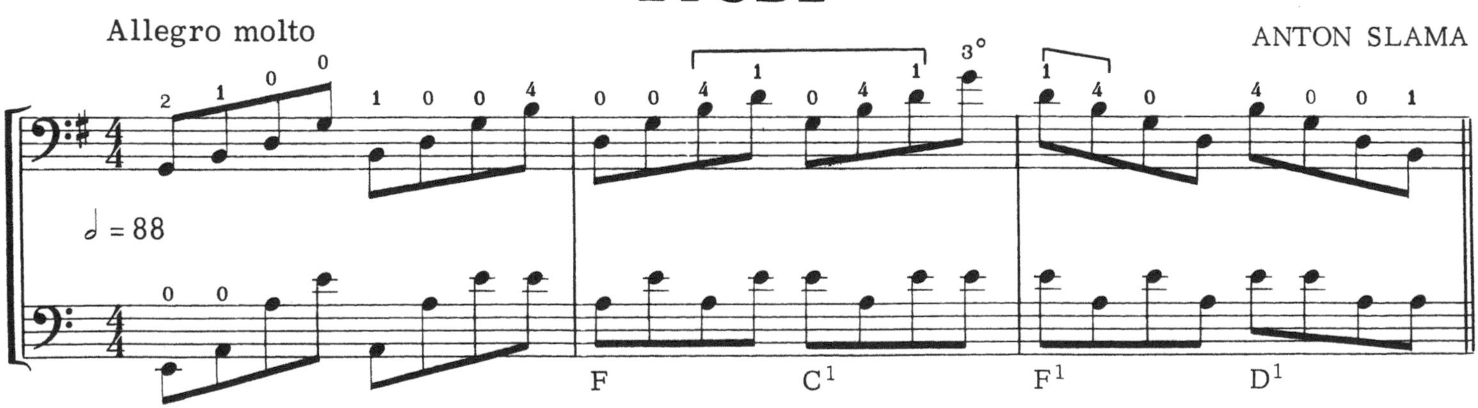

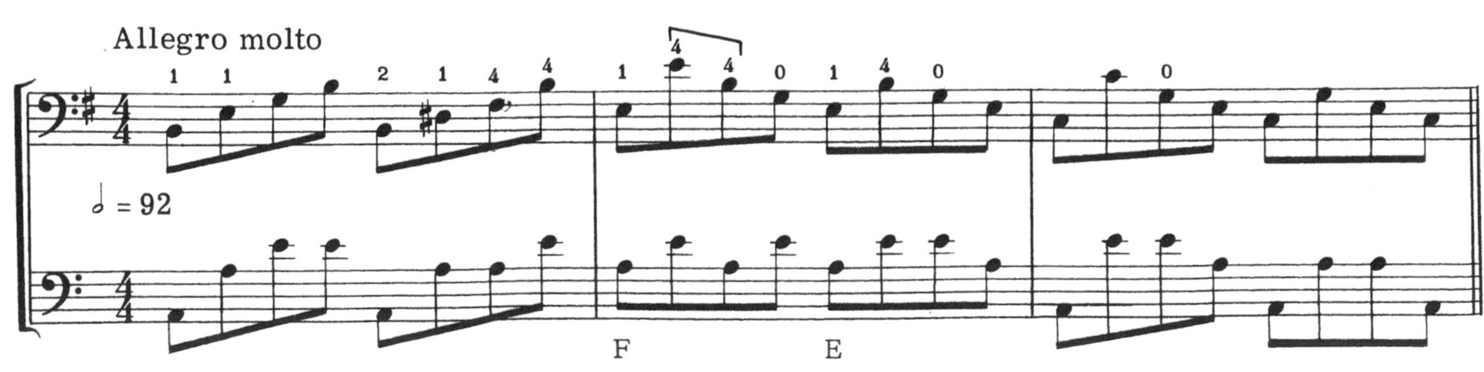

SONATA No. 5

ANTONIO VIVALDI

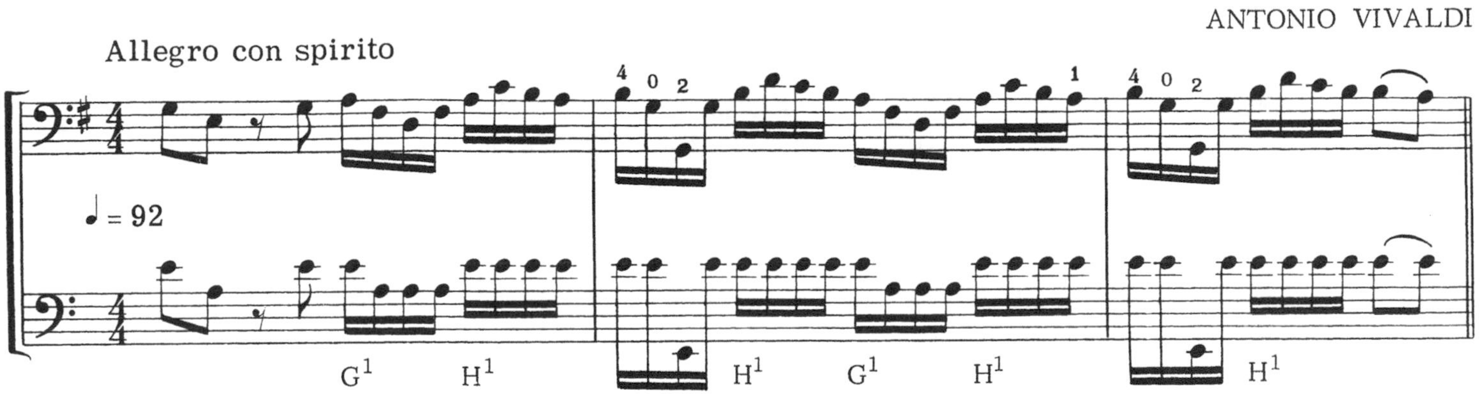

CARNIVAL OVERTURE

ANTON DVORAK

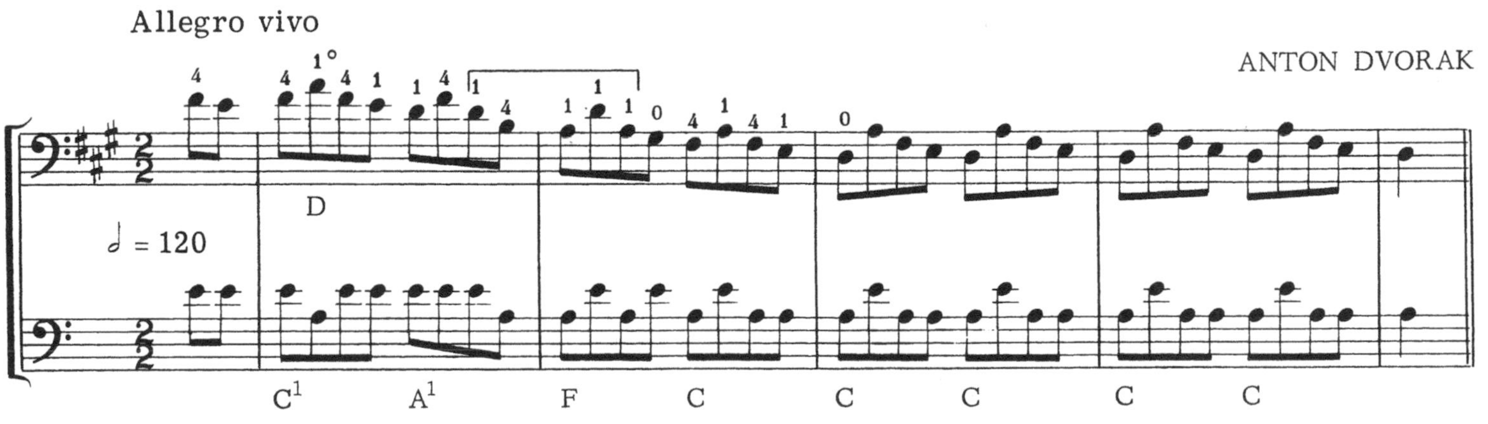

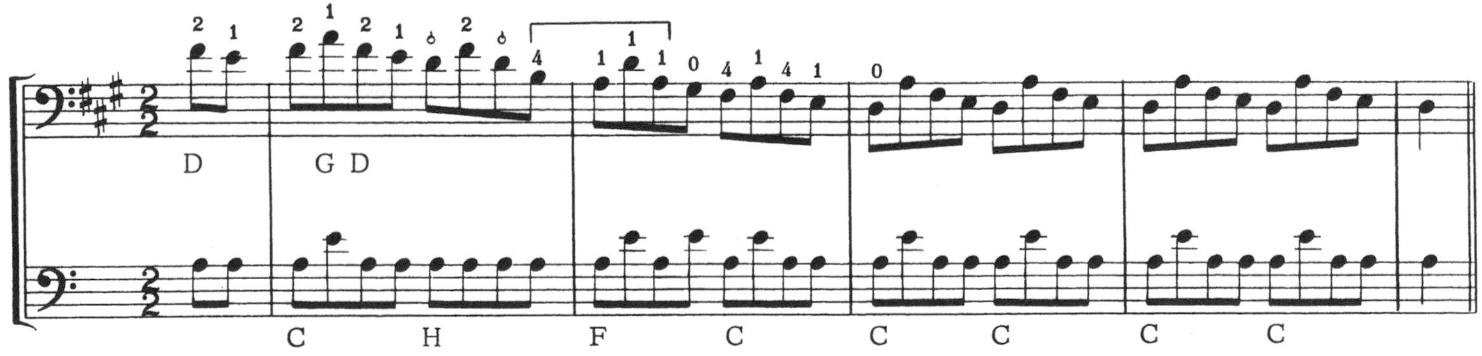

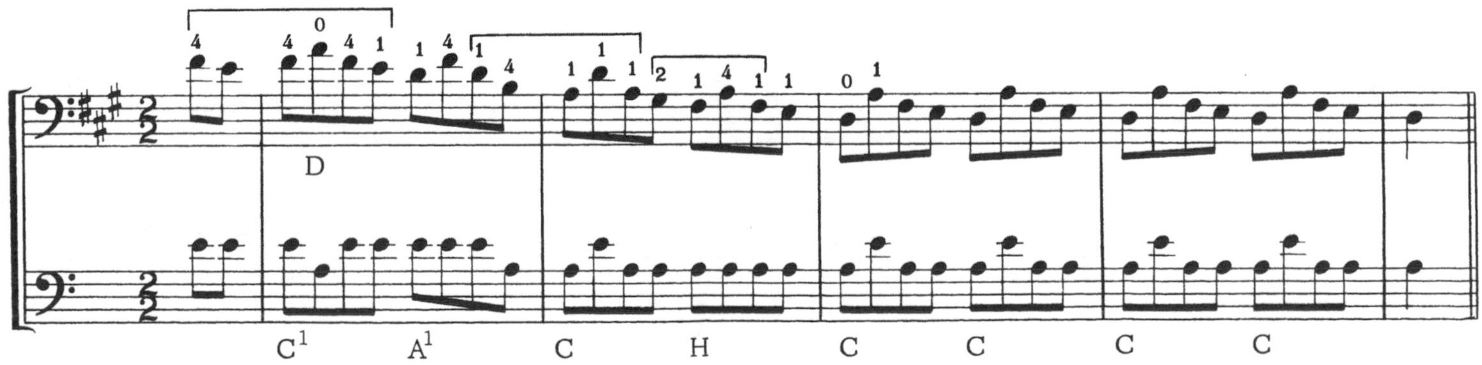

SYMPHONY FANTASTIQUE

HECTOR BERLIOZ

CONCERTO

DOMENICO DRAGONETTI

SYMPHONY No. 6

PETER I. TCHAIKOVSKY

SYMPHONY No. 88

JOSEPH HAYDN

SYMPHONY No. 5

SYMPHONY No. 3

LUDWIG VAN BEETHOVEN

Presto

♩ = 112

sf

B F¹ D C¹ A¹ H¹ A¹

SYMPHONY No. 5

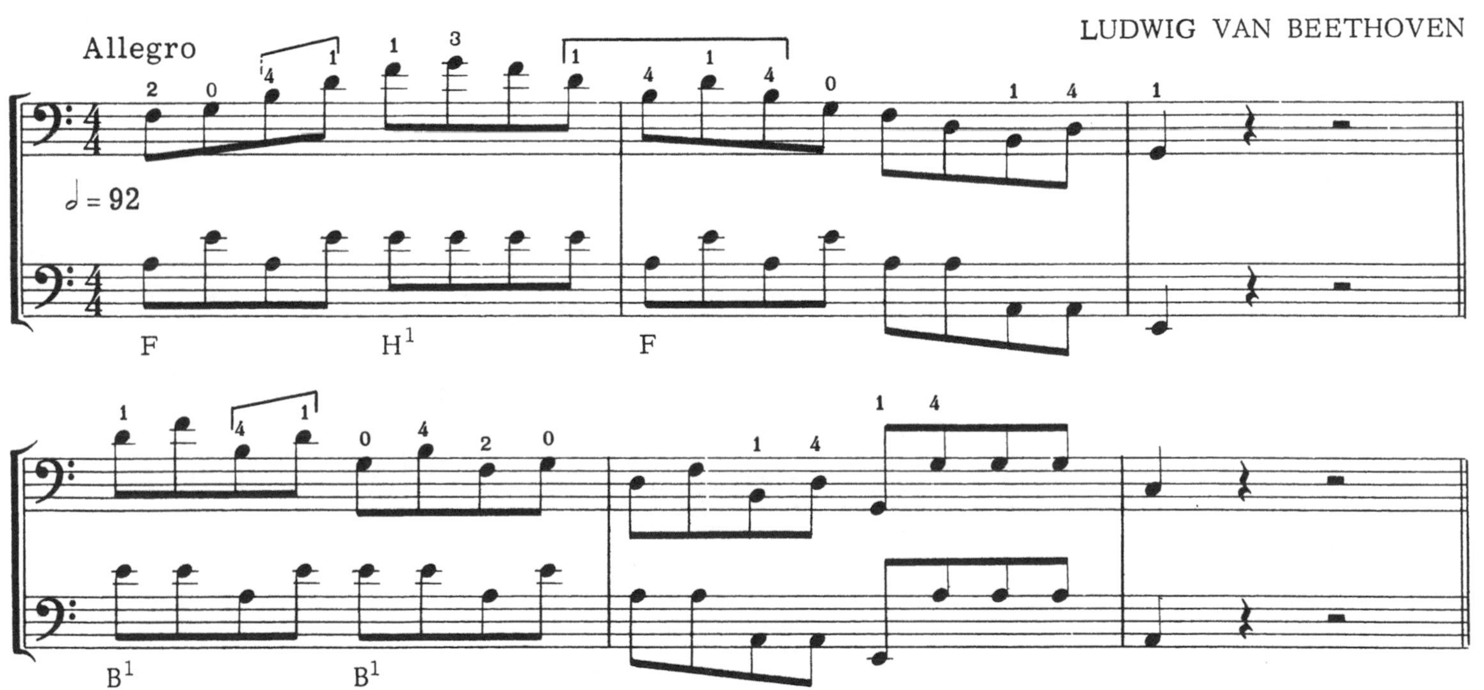

SYMPHONY No. 8 (Unfinished)

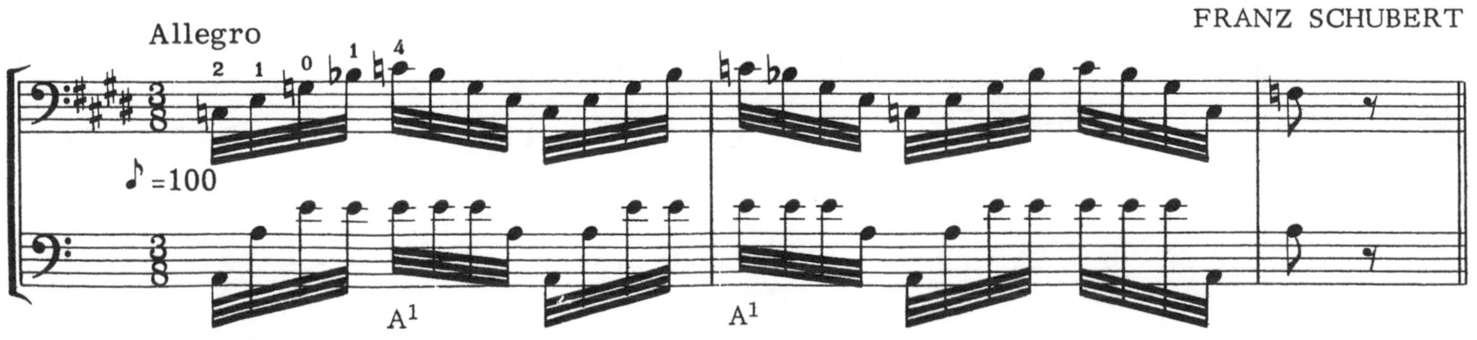

SYMPHONY No. 7

This bowing *(Piqué)* is to be played in the upper half of the bow; the dotted eighth note short *(Martelé)* and the sixteenth note with a smoother stroke *(Détaché)*.

SYMPHONY No. 41

WOLFGANG A. MOZART

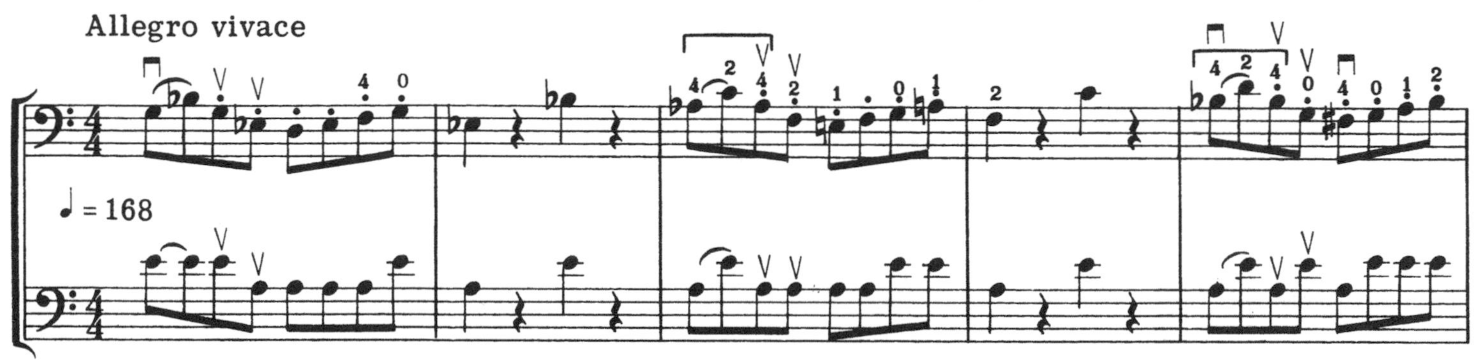

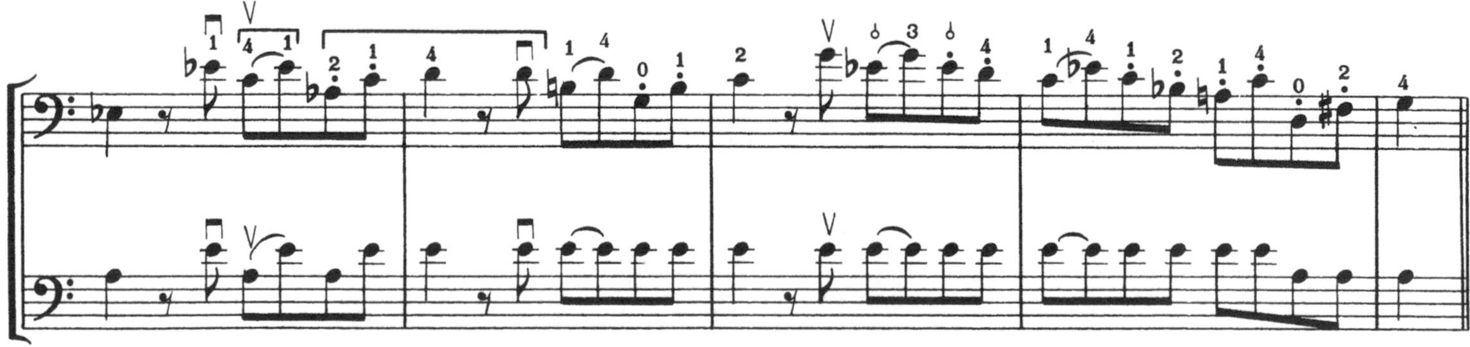

SONATA

for Two Violins, Cello and Double Bass

GIOACCHINO ROSSINI

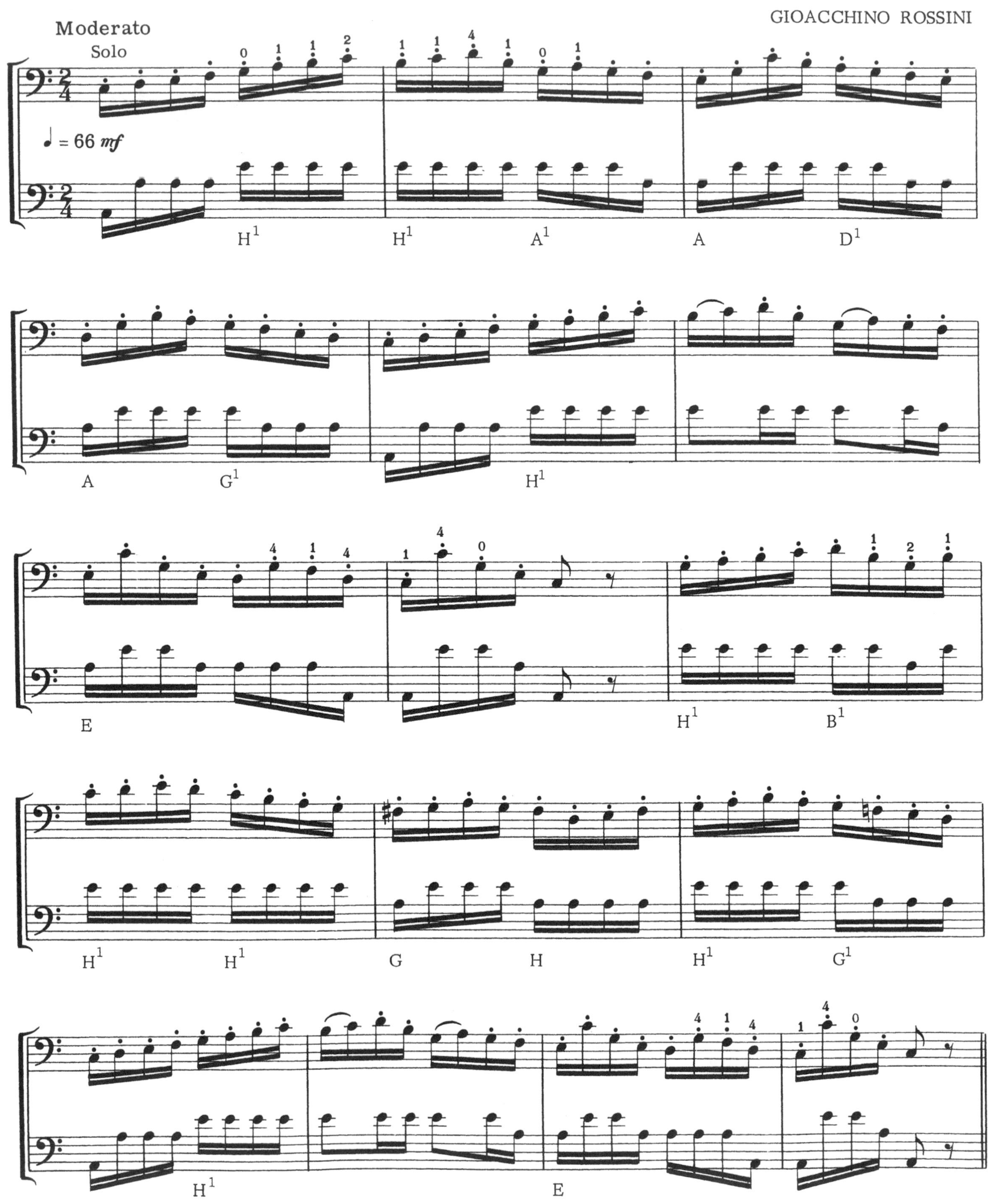

♪ = 60
f
A B C D1 E1 F G H1 I1a
B C D E F G H I b

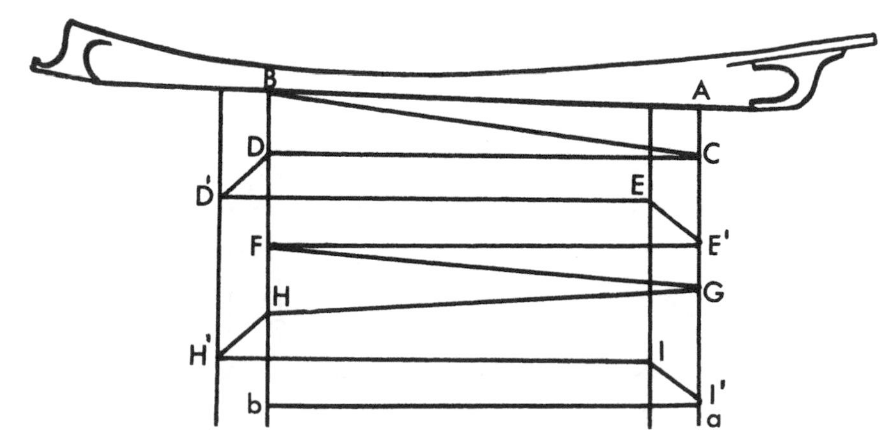
B
A
D
C
D'
E
F
E'
H
G
H'
I
I'
b
a

♪ = 60
f
A B C1 D1 E F G1 H1 a
B C D E F G H I b

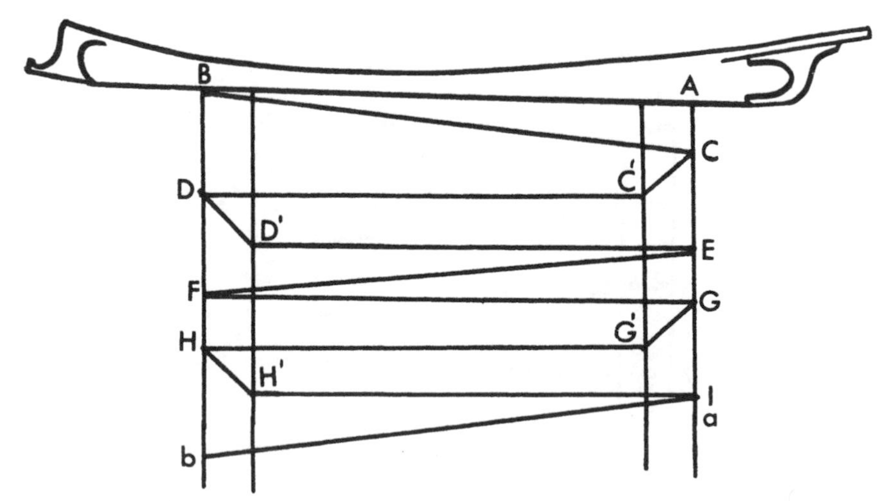
B
A
C
C'
D
D'
E
F
G
G'
H
H'
I
a
b

♪ = 60
f
A B1 C1 D E F1 G1 H a
B C D E F G H I b

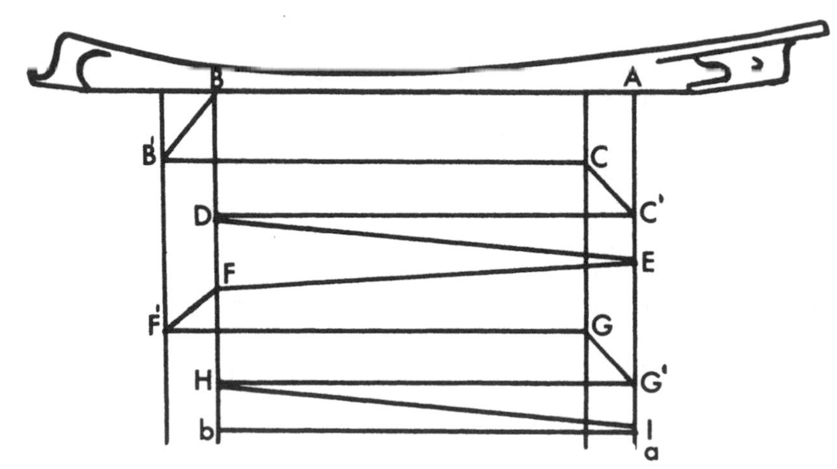
B
A
B'
C
D
C'
E
F
F'
G
H
G'
b
I
a

♪ = 60
f
A B C1 D E1 F G1 H I1 a
B C D E F G H I b

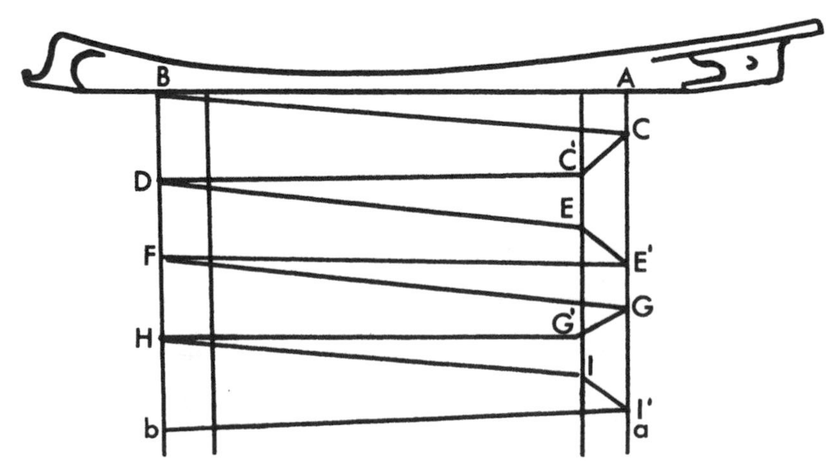
B
A
C
C'
D
E
F
E'
G
G'
H
I
I'
b
a

♪ = 60
f
A B
B¹ C
C D
D¹ E
E F
F¹ G
G H
H¹ I
a b

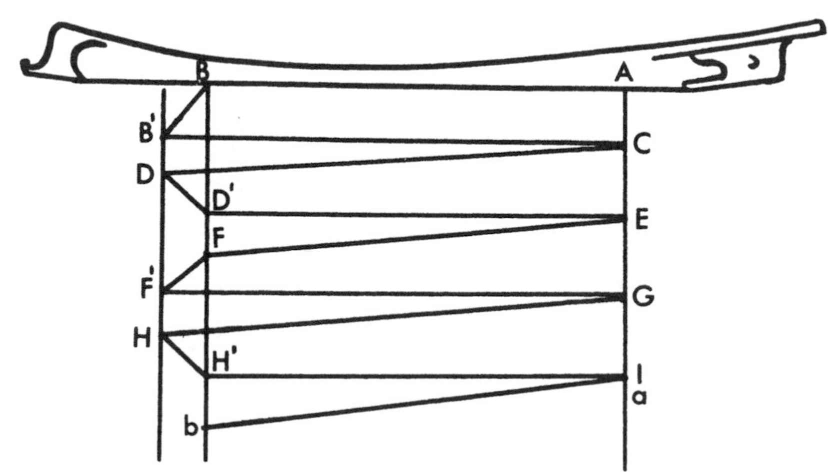
B
A
B'
C
D
D'
E
F
F'
G
H
H'
I
a
b

♪ = 60
f
A B
B¹ C
C¹ D
D¹ E
E¹ F
F¹ G
G¹ H
H¹ I
I¹a b

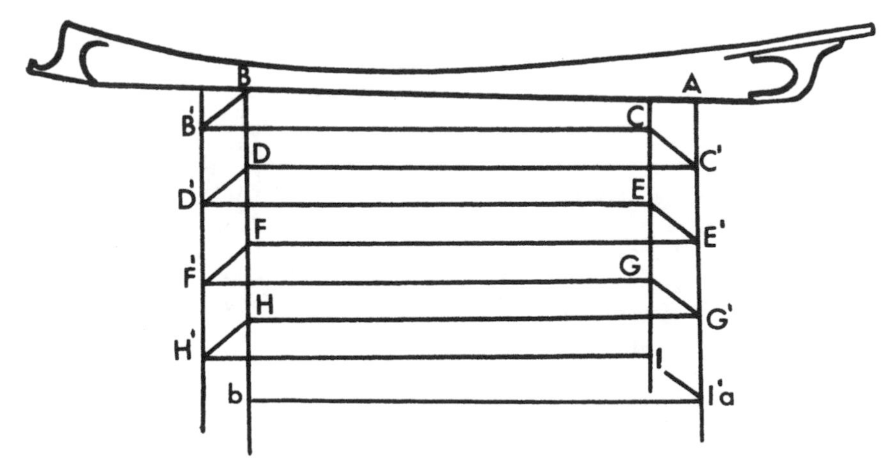
B
A
B'
C
C'
D
D'
E
E'
F
F'
G
G'
H
H'
I
I'a
b

♪= 176
f
A B^1 C^1 D^1 E^1 F^1 G^1 H^1 I^1a
B C D E F G H I

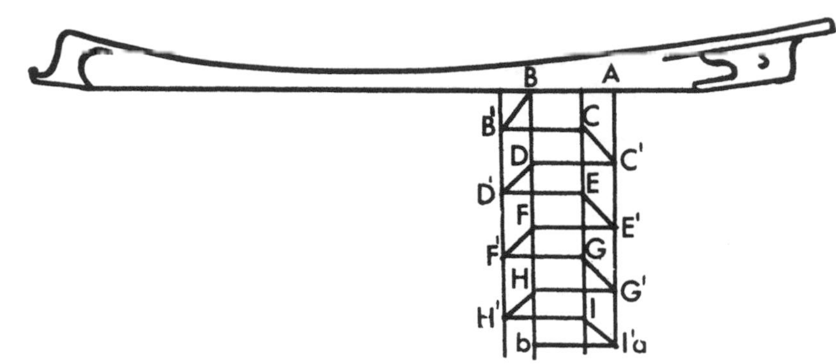
B A
B' C
D C'
D' E
F E'
F' G
H G'
H' I
b I'a

♩= 144
f
A B^1 C^1 D^1 E^1 F^1 G^1 H^1 I^1a
B C D E F G H I

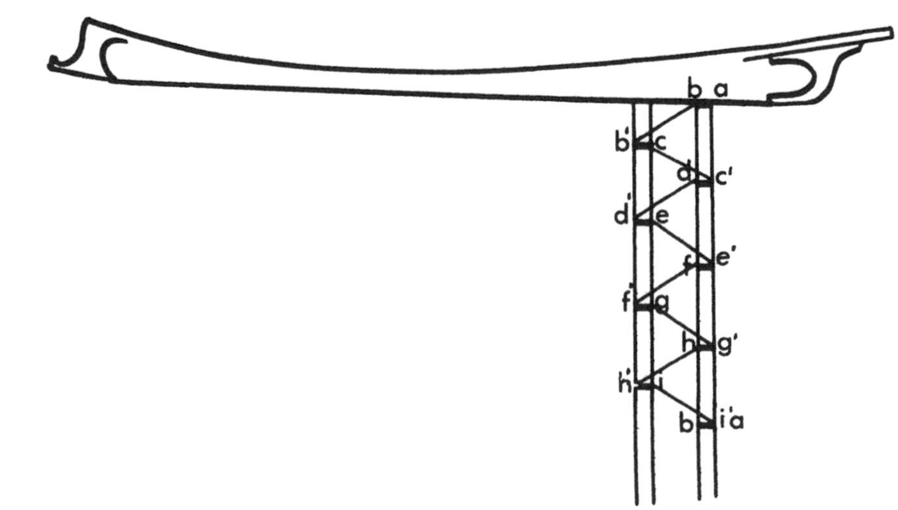
b a
b' c
d c'
d' e
f e'
f' g
h g'
h' i
b i'a

♪ = 60
f
A B1 C D E1 F1 G H I1a
B C D E F G H I b

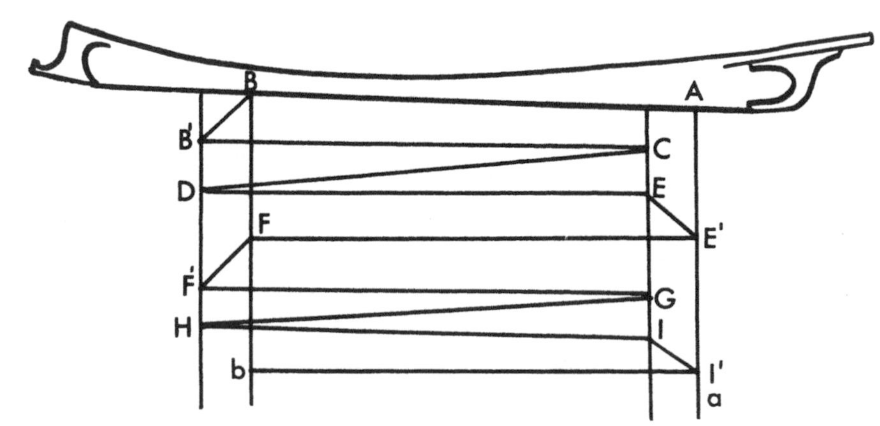
B
A
B'
C
D
E
F
E'
F'
G
H
I
b
I'
a

♪ = 60
f
A B C D E F G H a
B C D E F G H I b

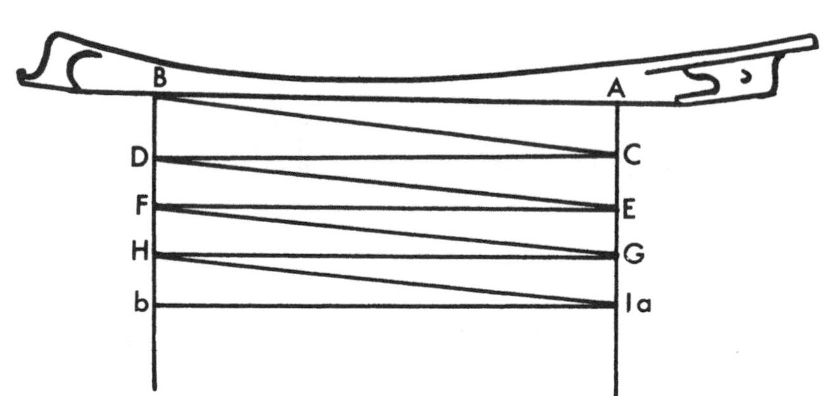
B
A
D
C
F
E
H
G
b
I a

SECTION II

PATTERN I

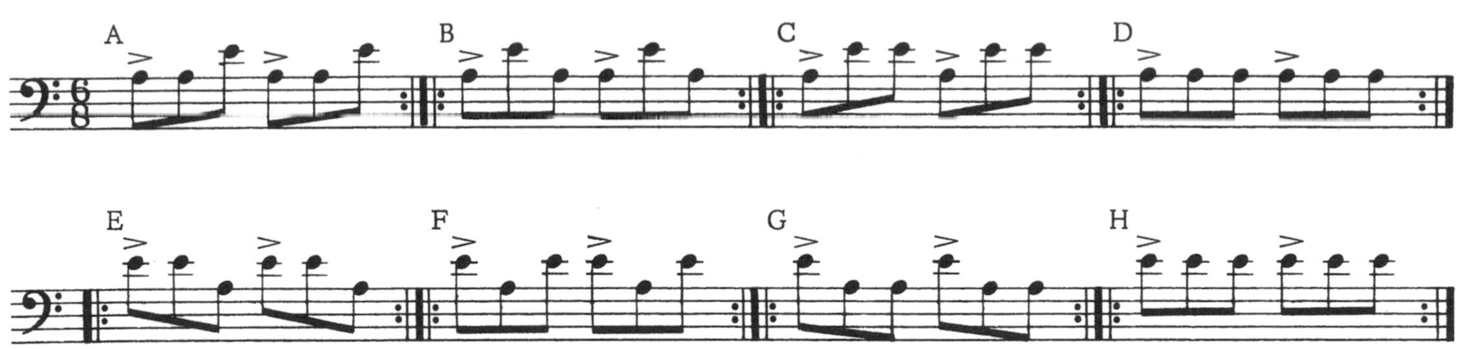

SUGGESTED PROCEDURE FOR PRACTICE

♩. = 92 to ♩. = 108 on the string - *détaché*.
♩. = 116 to ♩. = 152 *spiccato.*
♩. = 160 on the string.

ETUDE

PATTERN I

Allegro ♩. = 88 *(détaché)* ♩. = 112 *(spiccato)*

Allegro ♪. = 88

BOWINGS

PATTERN I

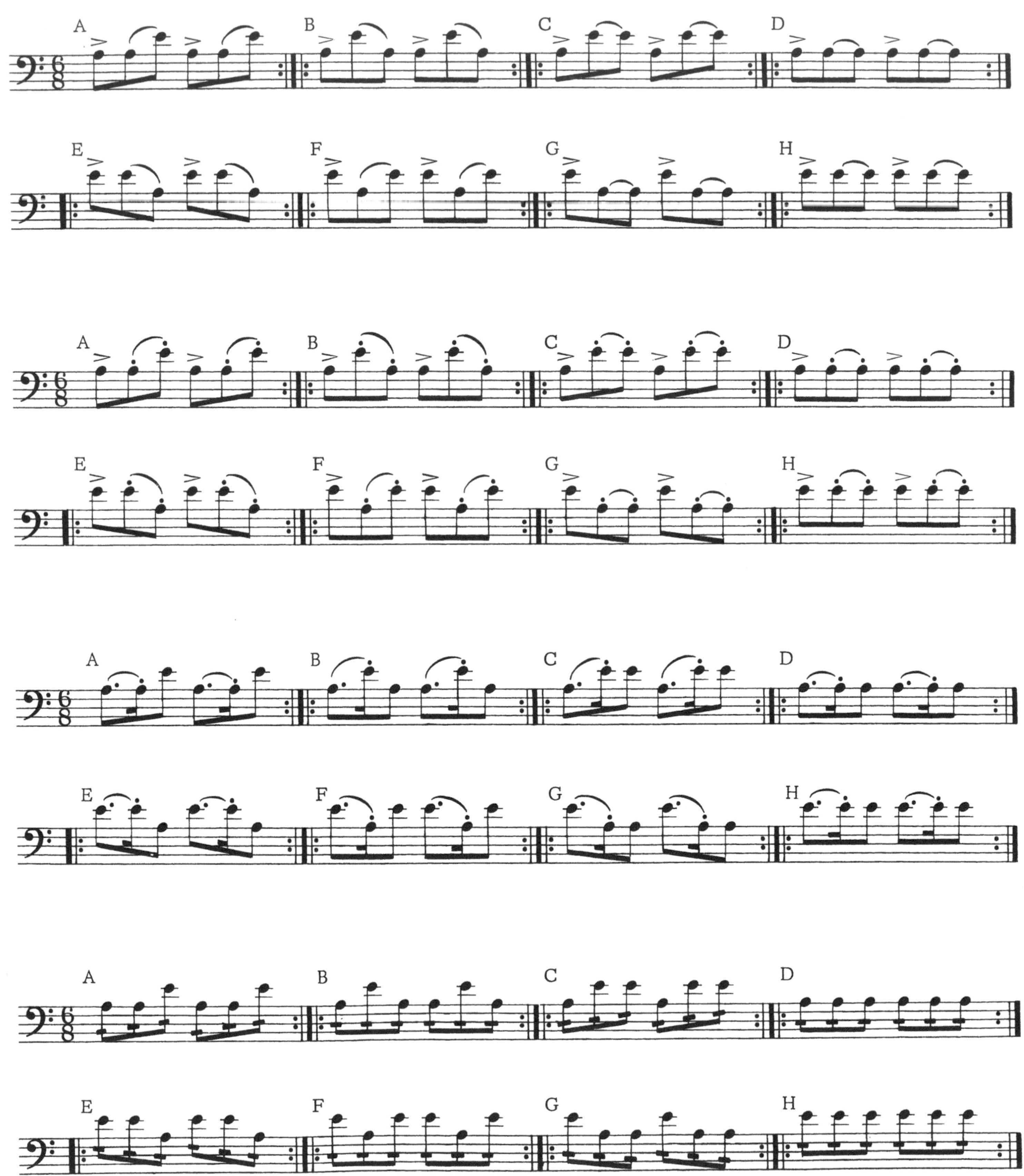

ETUDES

BOWINGS (PATTERN I)

PERMUTATIONS OF PATTERN I

E
A
E
B
E
C
E
D
E
F
E
G
E
H
F
A
F
B
F
C
F
D
F
E
F
G
F
H
G
A
G
B
G
C
G
D
G
E
G
F
G
H
H
A
H
B
H
C
H
D
H
E
H
F
H
G

ETUDES

PERMUTATIONS OF PATTERN I

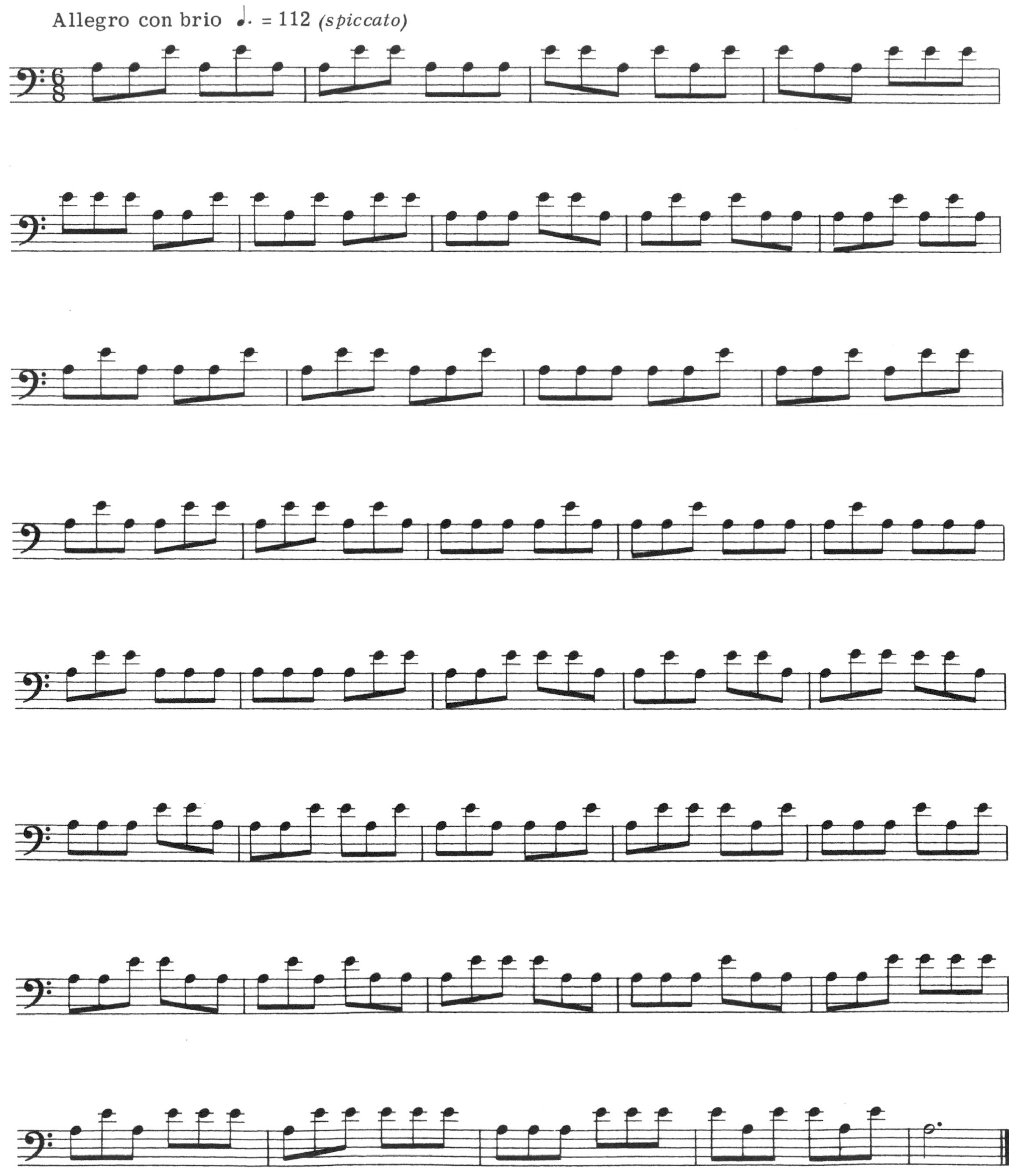

This exercise is to be practiced with a *Martelé* bowing; each note beginning with a sharp attack and separated from the next note.

Allegro non troppo ♩. = 88

ETUDES

BOWINGS (PERMUTATIONS OF PATTERN I)

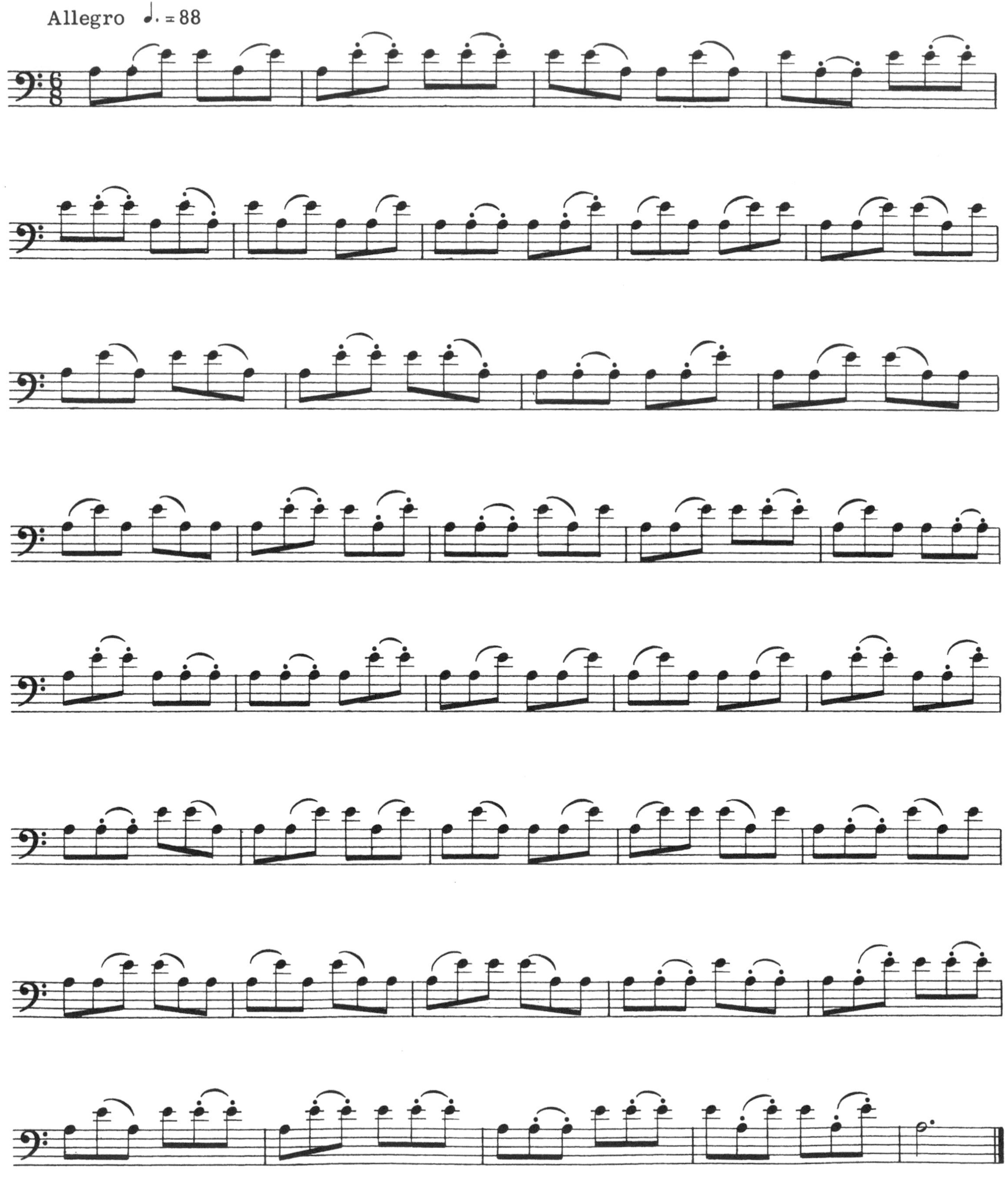

Allegro ♩. = 96

Moderato ♩. = 76

VARIATION OF PATTERN I

PERMUTATIONS

D
A
D
B
D
C
D
E
D
F
D
G
D
H
E
A
E
B
E
C
E
D
E
F
E
G
E
H
F
A
F
B
F
C
F
D
F
E
F
G
F
H
G
A
G
B
G
C
G
D
G
E
G
F
G
H

ETUDE

PERMUTATIONS OF VARIATIONS OF PATTERN I

Moderato ♩. = 76

ETUDES

PERMUTATIONS OF ANOTHER VARIATION OF PATTERN I

EXERCISES BASED ON PATTERN I

Allegro di bravura ♩. = 132

TROUT - QUINTET

SYMPHONY No. 4 (Italian)

Allegro vivace

FELIX MENDELSSOHN

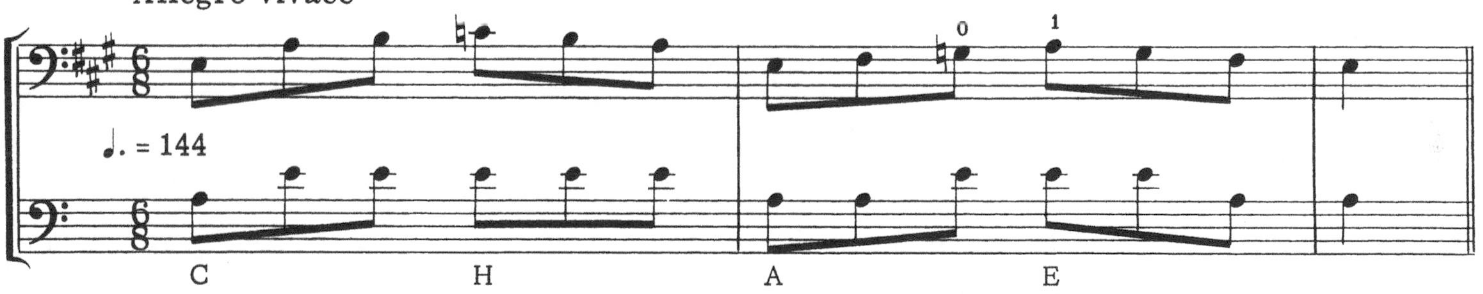

♩. = 144

C H A E

Allegro vivace

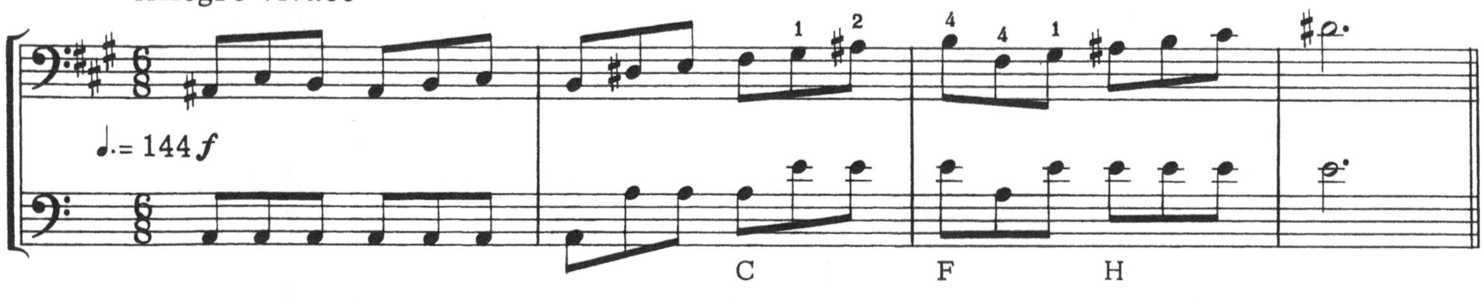

♩. = 144 *f*

C F H

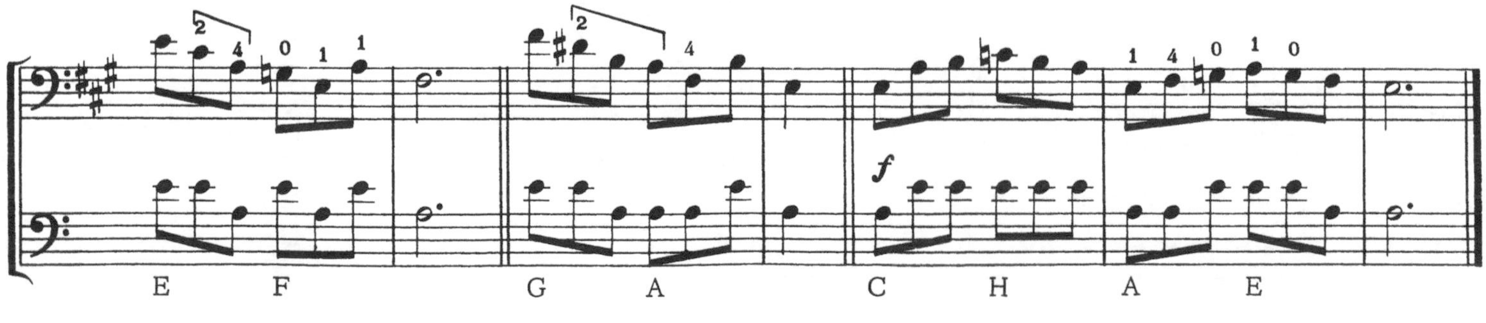

f

E F G A C H A E

OVERTURE TO "EURYANTHE"

CARL MARIA von WEBER

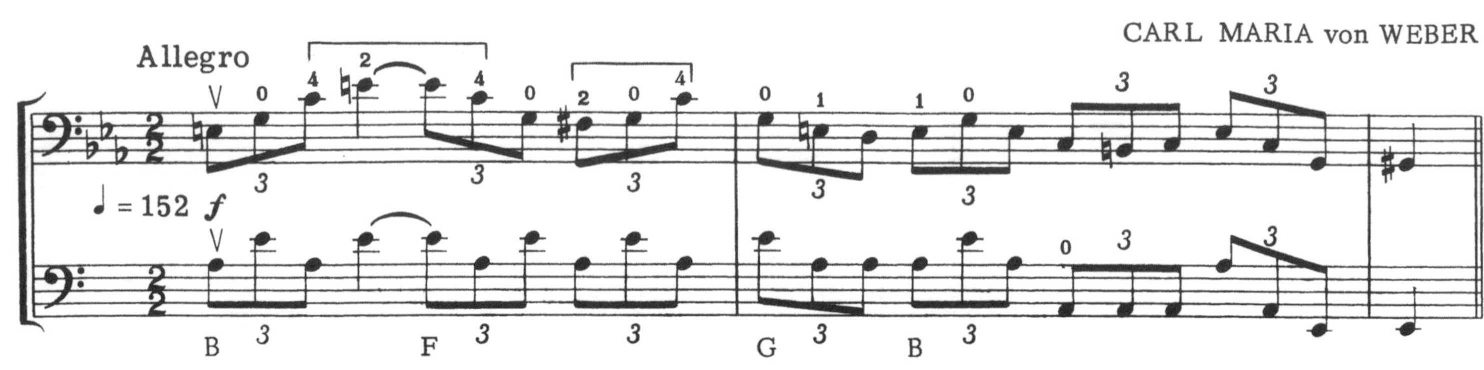

SYMPHONY No. 103 (Drum Roll)

JOSEPH HAYDN

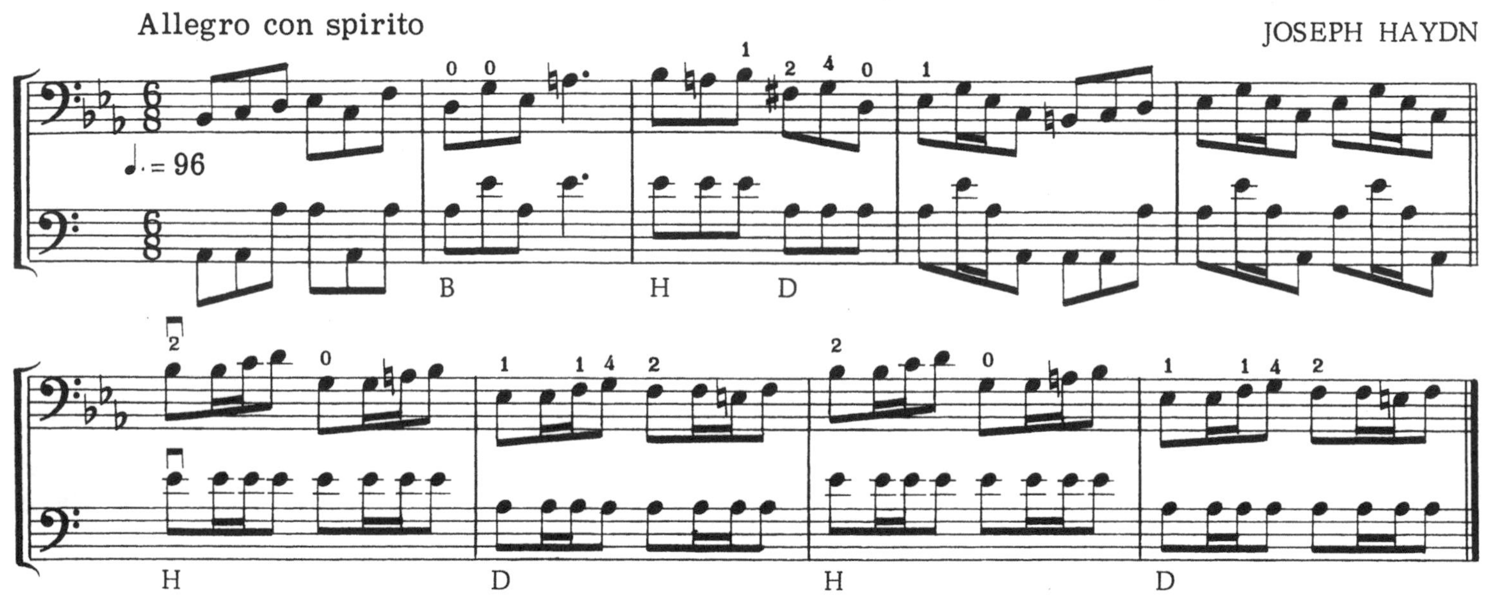

SYMPHONY No. 5

PETER I. TCHAIKOVSKY

CEPHALE ET PROCRIS SUITE

SYMPHONY No. 7

LUDWIG VAN BEETHOVEN

PIANO CONCERTO No. 4

Presto

LUDWIG VAN BEETHOVEN

TILL EULENSPIEGEL

Allegro con brio

RICHARD STRAUSS

DON QUIXOTE

Allegro di molto

RICHARD STRAUSS

SYMPHONY No. 7

Allegro vivace (in one)

FRANZ SCHUBERT

SYMPHONY No. 1

Allegro

JOHANNES BRAHMS

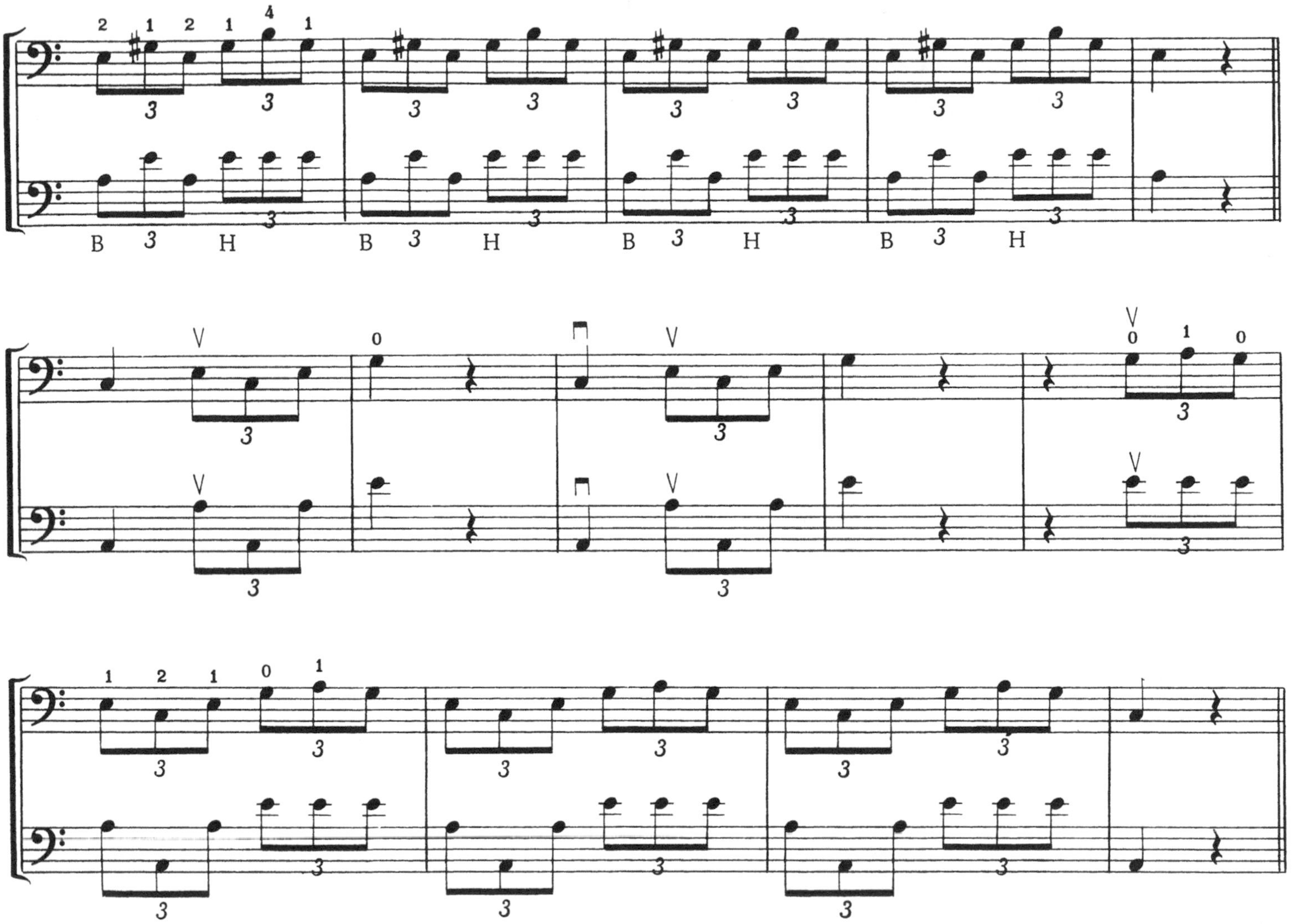

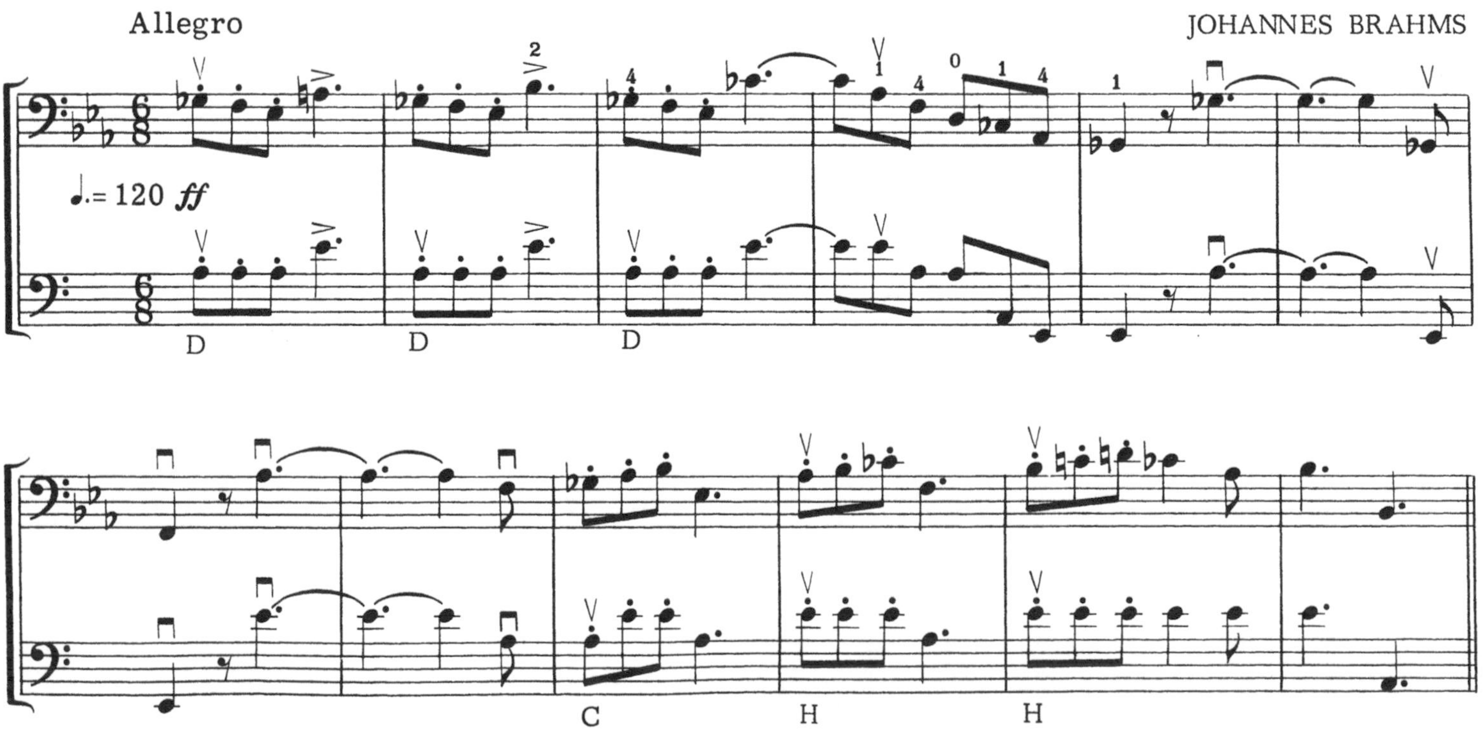

♪ = 50
f
A B C1 D1 E F1 G1a
B C D E F G b

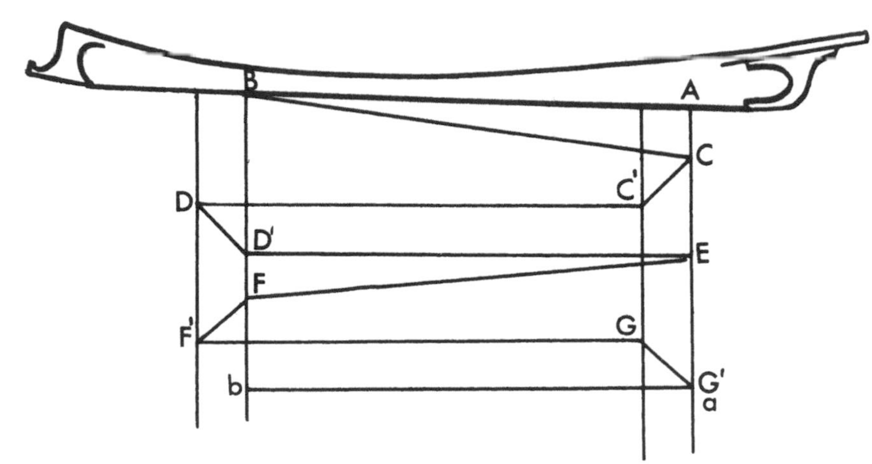
B
A
C
C'
D
D'
E
F
F'
G
b
G'
a

♪ = 50
f
A B1 C1 D E1 F1 Ga
B C D E F G b

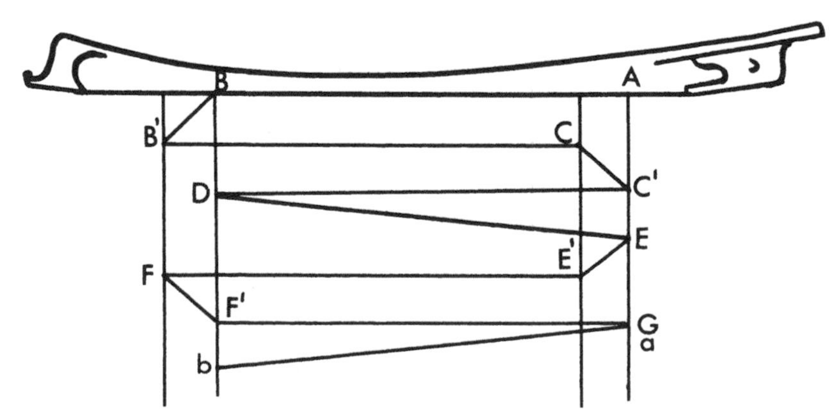
B
A
B'
C
C'
D
E
E'
F
F'
G
a
b

♪ = 50
f
A B¹ C D¹ E¹ F G¹a
B C D E F G b

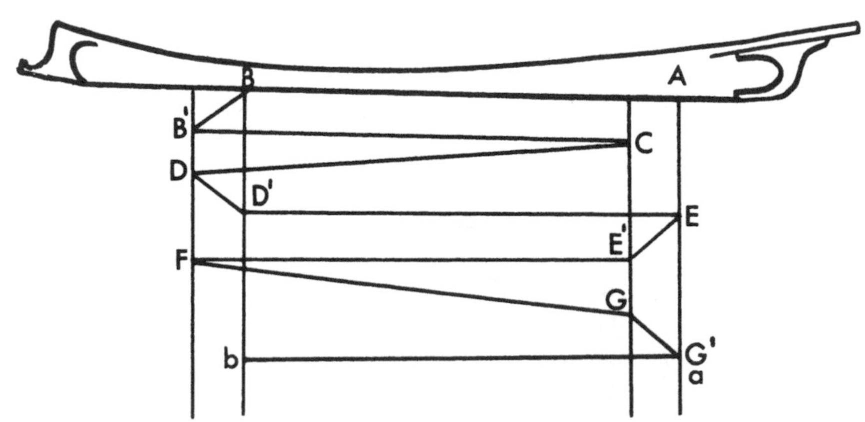
B
A
B'
C
D
D'
E
E'
F
G
G'
a
b

♪ = 50
f
A B C D E F Ga
B C D E F G b

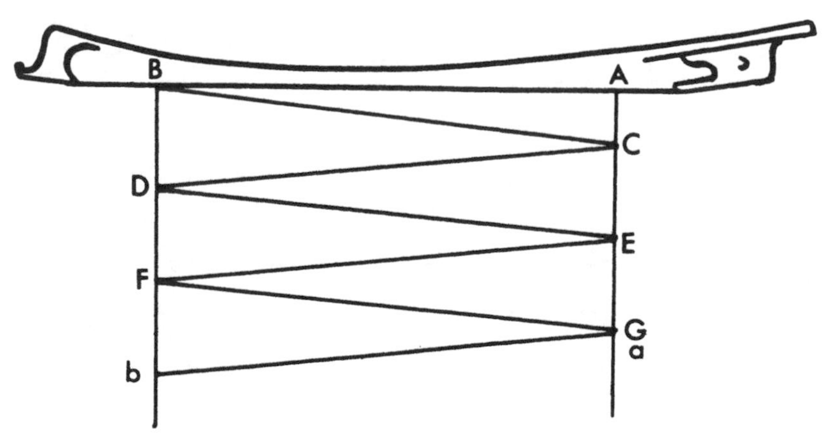
B
A
C
D
E
F
G
a
b

♪ = 50
f
A B C1 D1 E F1 G1a
B C D E F G b

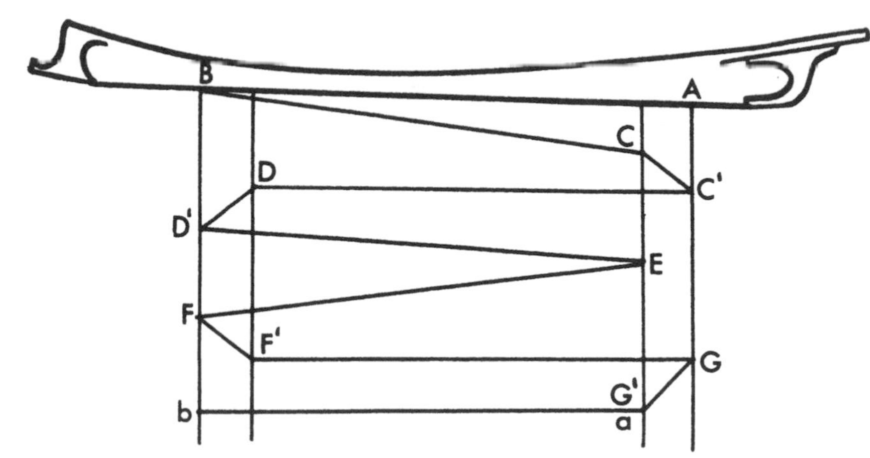
B
A
C
D
C'
D'
E
F
F'
G
G'
b
a

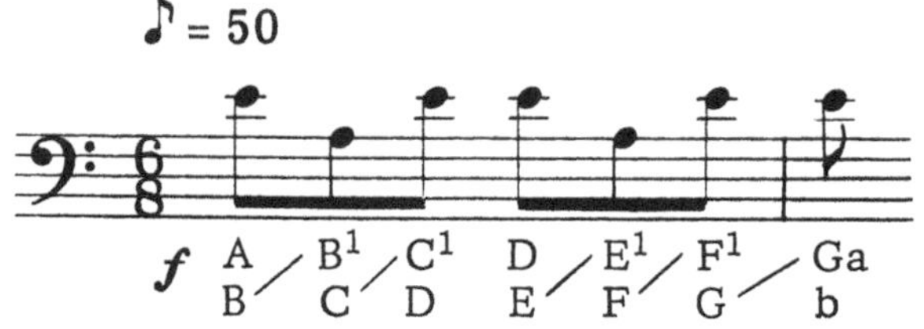
♪ = 50
f
A B1 C1 D E1 F1 Ga
B C D E F G b

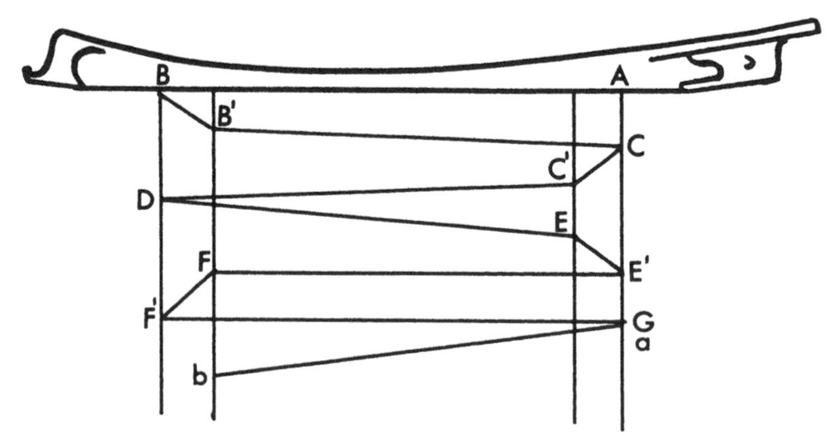
B
A
B'
C
C'
D
E
F
E'
F'
G
a
b

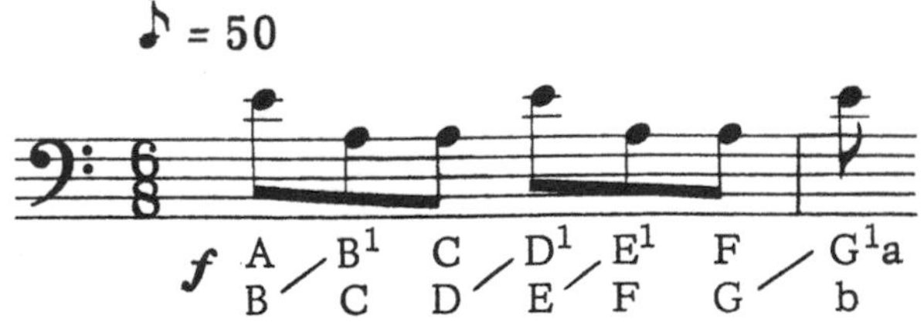
♪ = 50
f
A B¹ C D¹ E¹ F G¹a
B C D E F G b

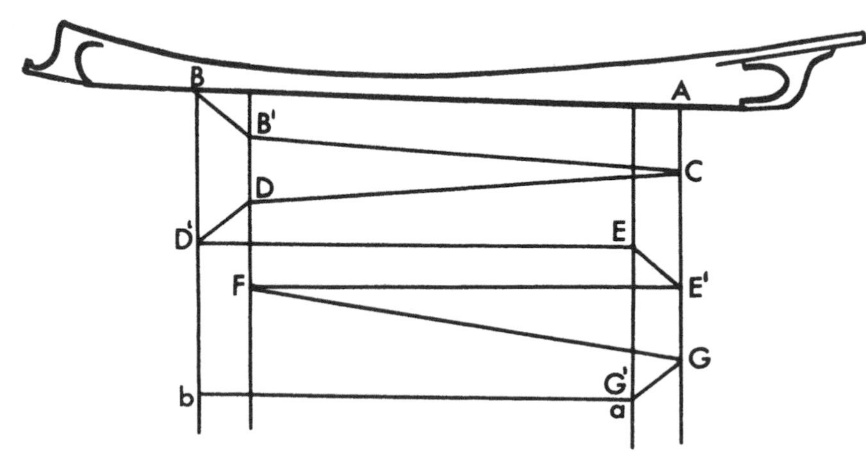
B
A
B'
C
D
D'
E
F
E'
G
G'
a
b

♪ = 50
f
A B C D E F
B C D E F G

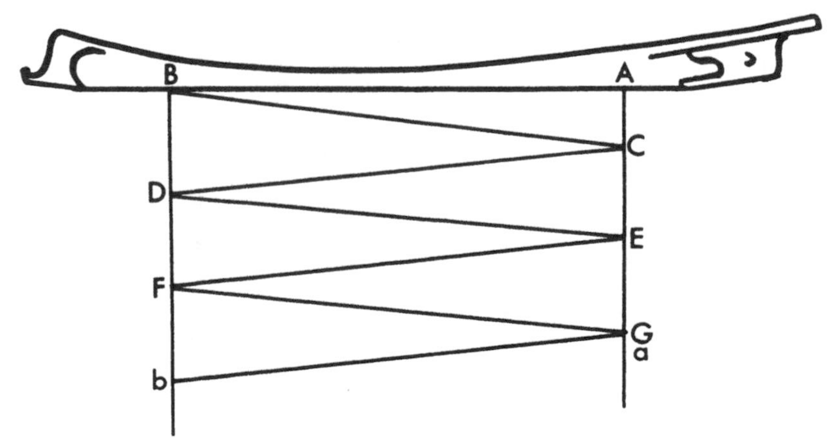
B
A
C
D
E
F
G
a
b

SECTION III

PATTERN I

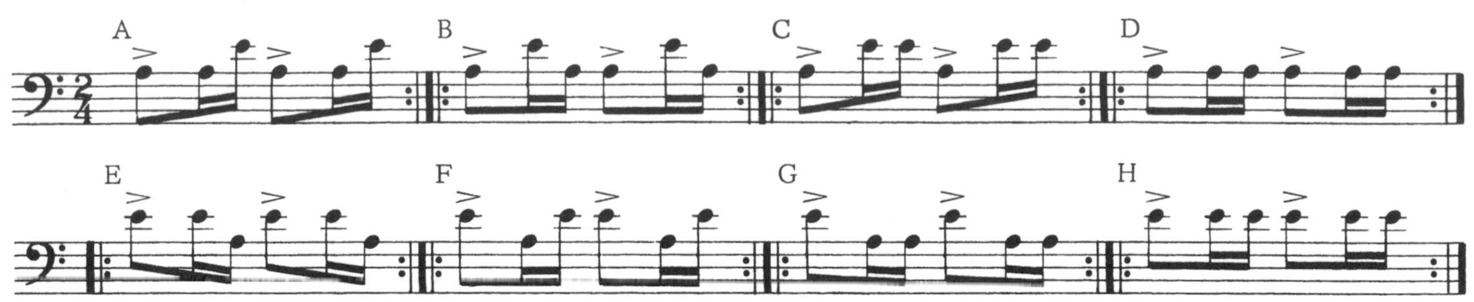

SUGGESTED PROCEDURE FOR PRACTICE

ETUDE

PATTERN I

PERMUTATIONS

PATTERN I

E A E B E C
E D E F E G E H
F A F B F C
F D F E F G F H
G A G B G C
G D G E G F G H
H A H B H C
H D H E H F H G

ETUDES

PERMUTATIONS OF PATTERN I

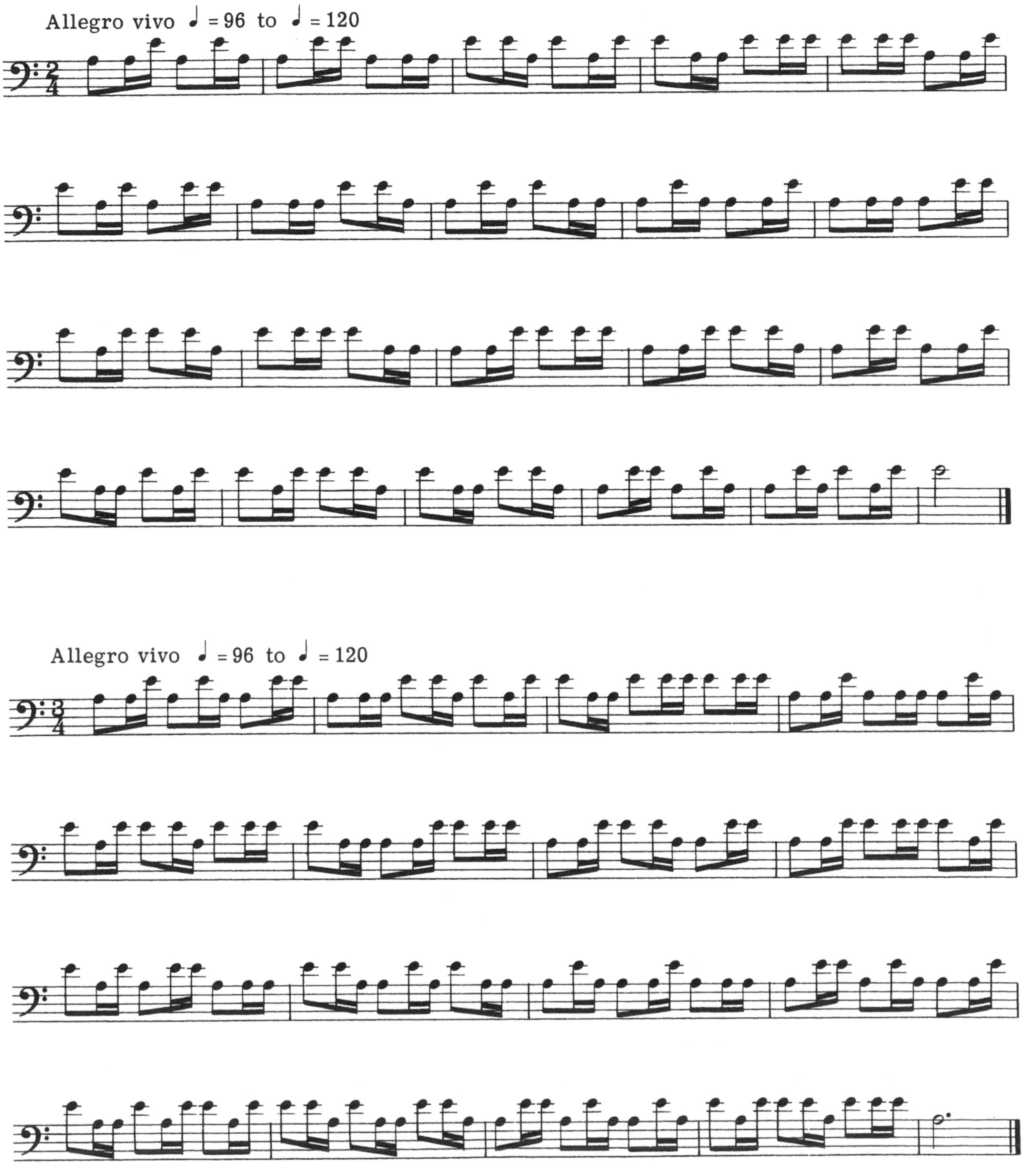

BOWINGS

PATTERN I

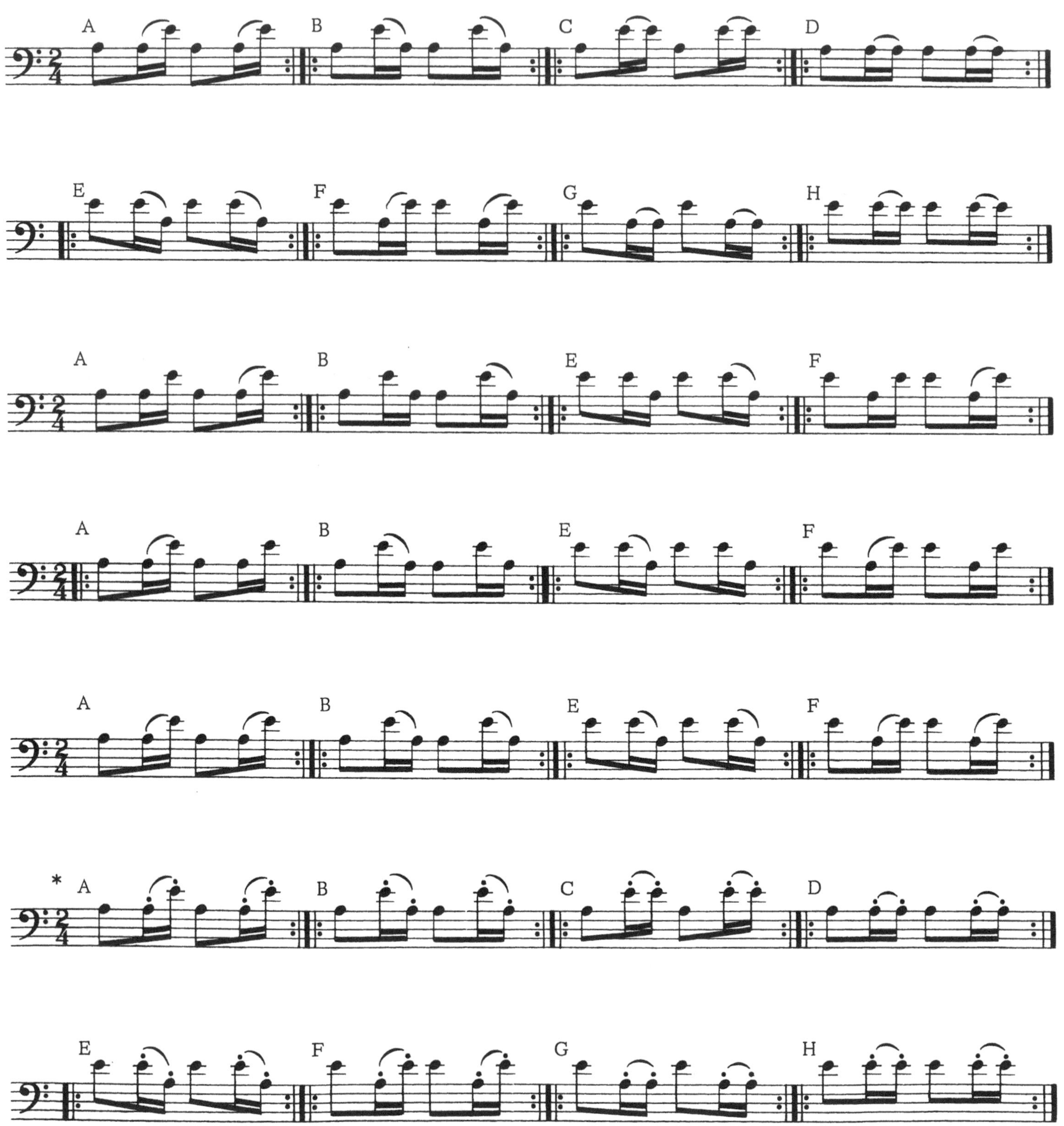

* The dotted notes are to be played alternately on the string *(Staccato)* and off the string *(Flying Spiccato)*.

ETUDE

BOWINGS (PATTERN I)

ETUDE

BOWINGS (PERMUTATIONS OF PATTERN I)

PATTERN II

PERMUTATIONS OF PATTERN II

E^1 A^1 E^1 B^1 E^1 C^1
E^1 D^1 E^1 F^1 E^1 G^1 E^1 H^1
F^1 A^1 F^1 B^1 F^1 C^1
F^1 D^1 F^1 E^1 F^1 G^1 F^1 H^1
G^1 A^1 G^1 B^1 G^1 C^1
G^1 D^1 G^1 E^1 G^1 F^1 G^1 H^1
H^1 A^1 H^1 B^1 H^1 C^1
H^1 D^1 H^1 E^1 H^1 F^1 H^1 G^1

ETUDE

PERMUTATIONS OF PATTERN II

PERMUTATIONS OF PATTERNS I & II

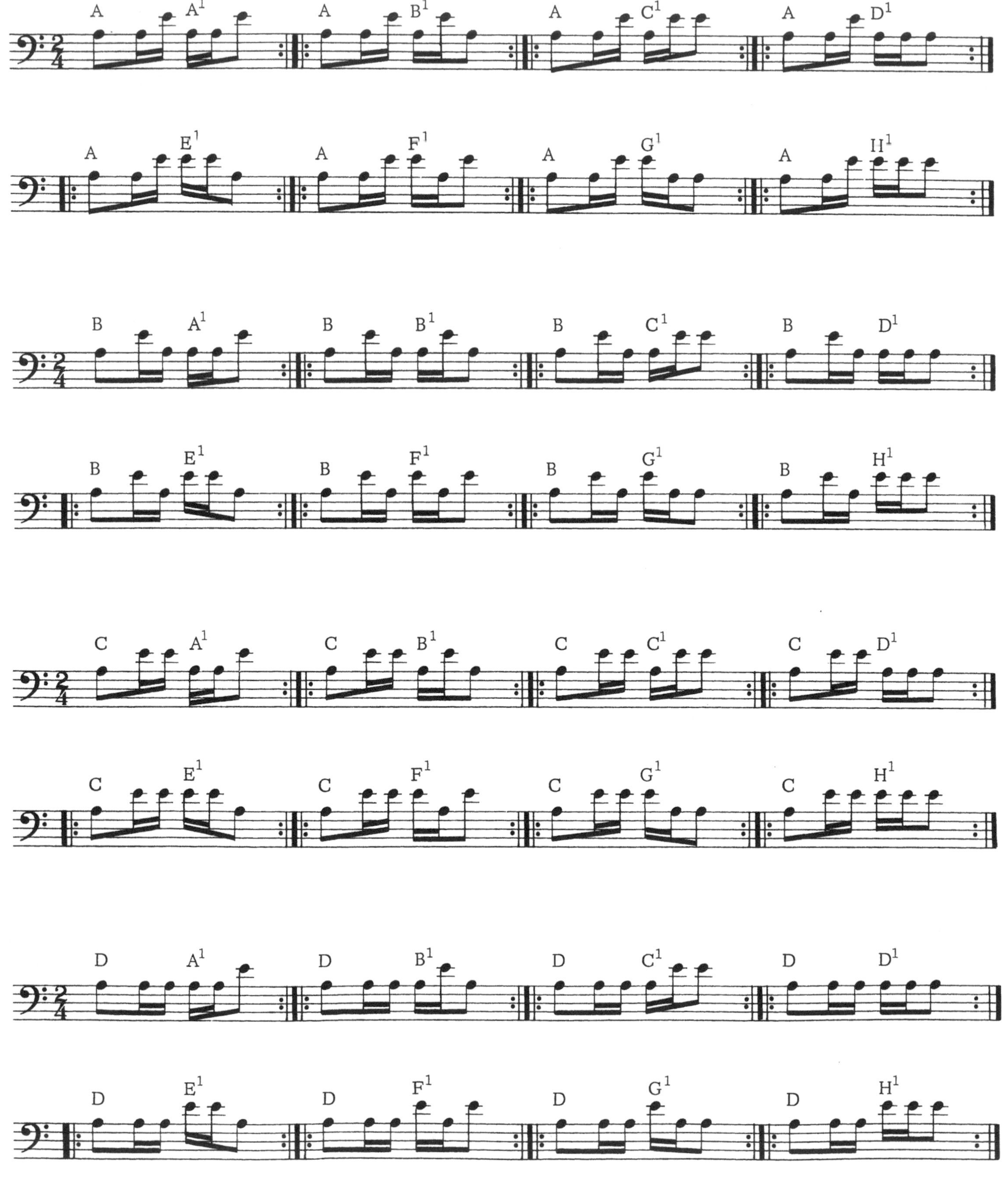

E
A1
E
B1
E
C1
E
D1
E
E1
E
F1
E
G1
E
H1
F
A1
F
B1
F
C1
F
D1
F
E1
F
F1
F
G1
F
H1
G
A1
G
B1
G
C1
G
D1
G
E1
G
F1
G
G1
G
H1
H
A1
H
B1
H
C1
H
D1
H
E1
H
F1
H
G1
H
H1

ETUDES

PERMUTATIONS OF PATTERNS I & II

Allegro ♩ = 92 to ♩ = 108

Allegro ♩ = 108

PERMUTATIONS OF PATTERNS II & I

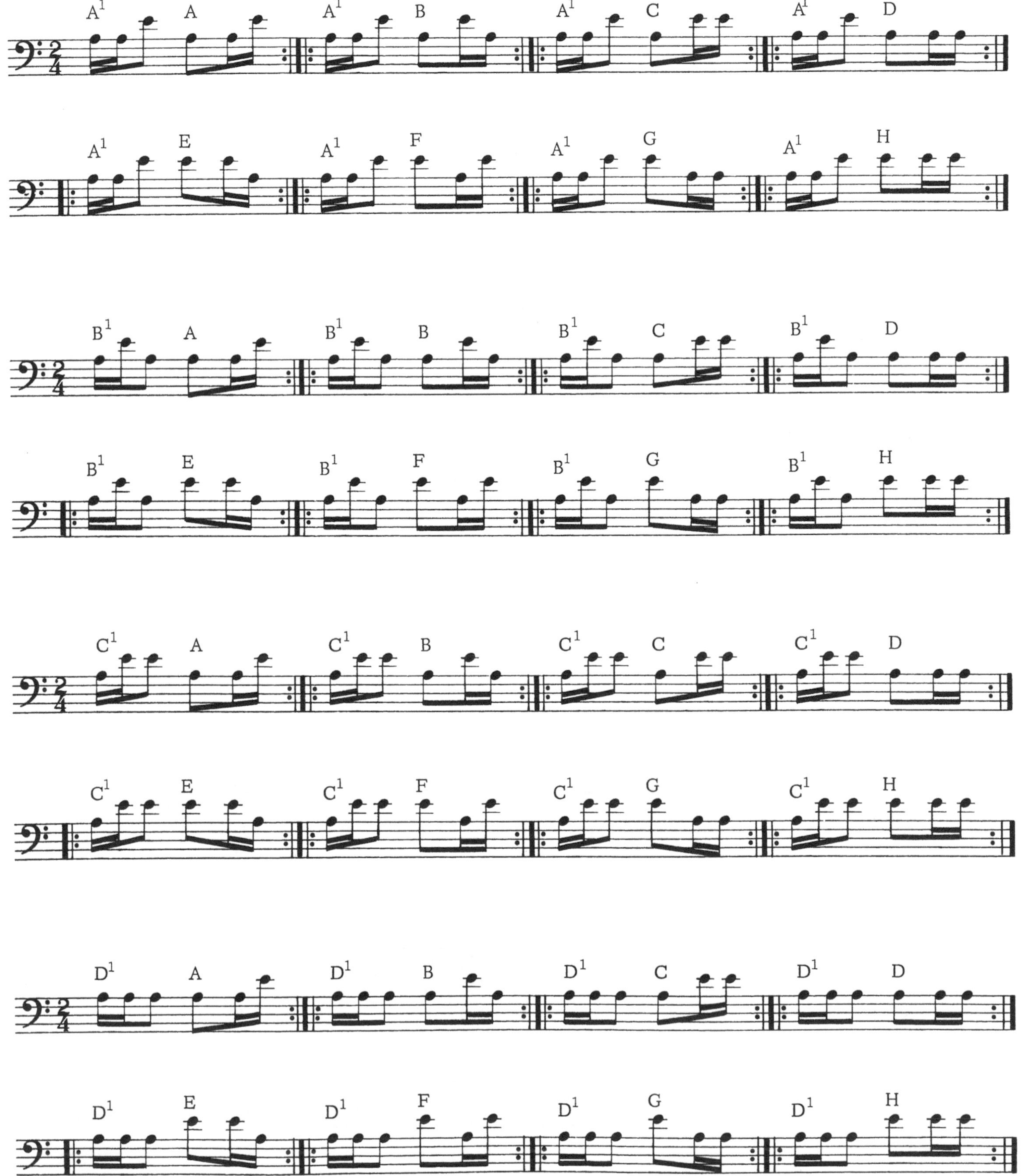

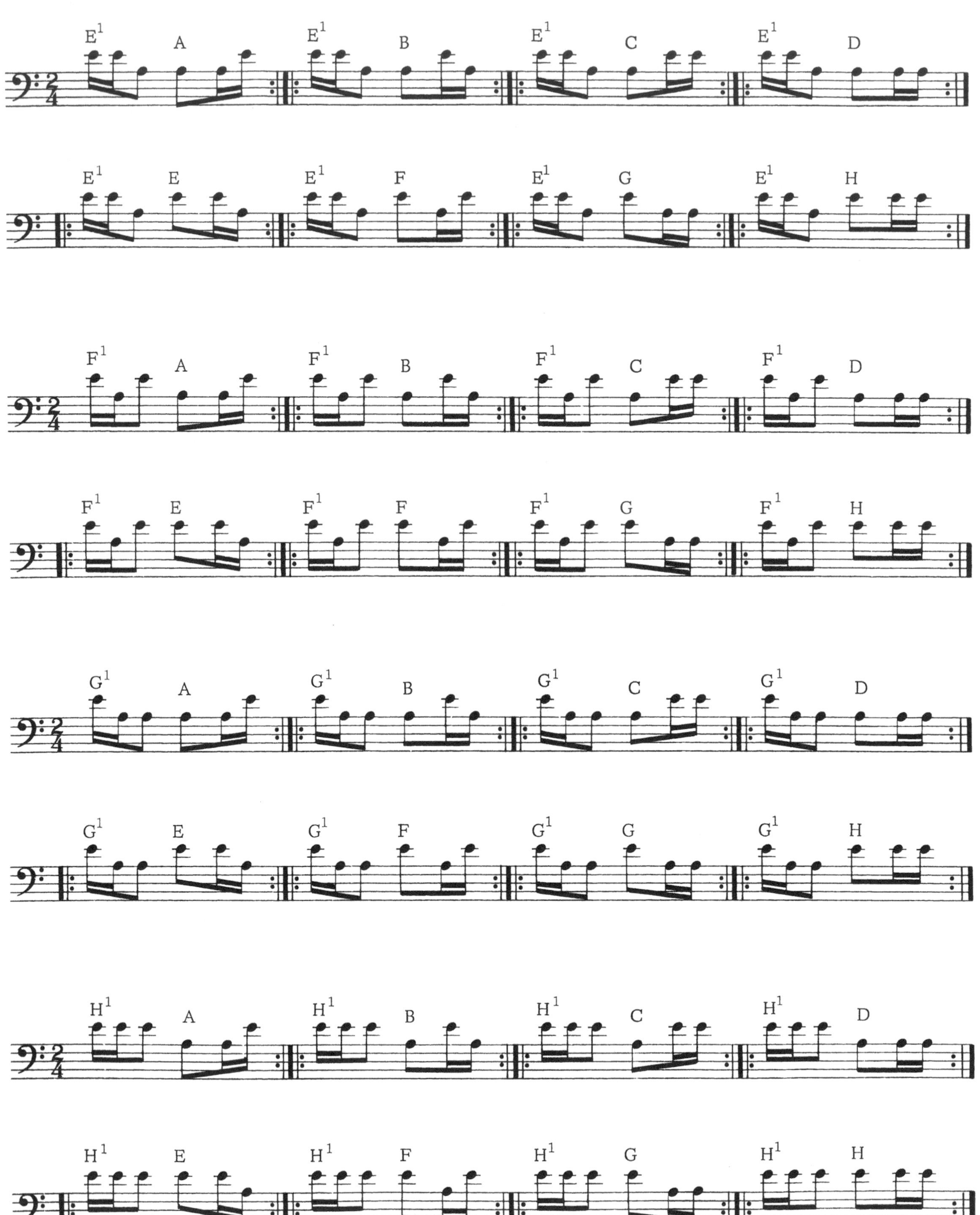
E1 A E1 B E1 C E1 D
E1 E E1 F E1 G E1 H
F1 A F1 B F1 C F1 D
F1 E F1 F F1 G F1 H
G1 A G1 B G1 C G1 D
G1 E G1 F G1 G G1 H
H1 A H1 B H1 C H1 D
H1 E H1 F H1 G H1 H

ETUDE

PERMUTATIONS OF PATTERNS II & I

Allegro con moto ♩ = 88 to ♩ = 100

VARIATIONS ON A THEME BY HAYDN

(Variation No.6)

JOHANNES BRAHMS

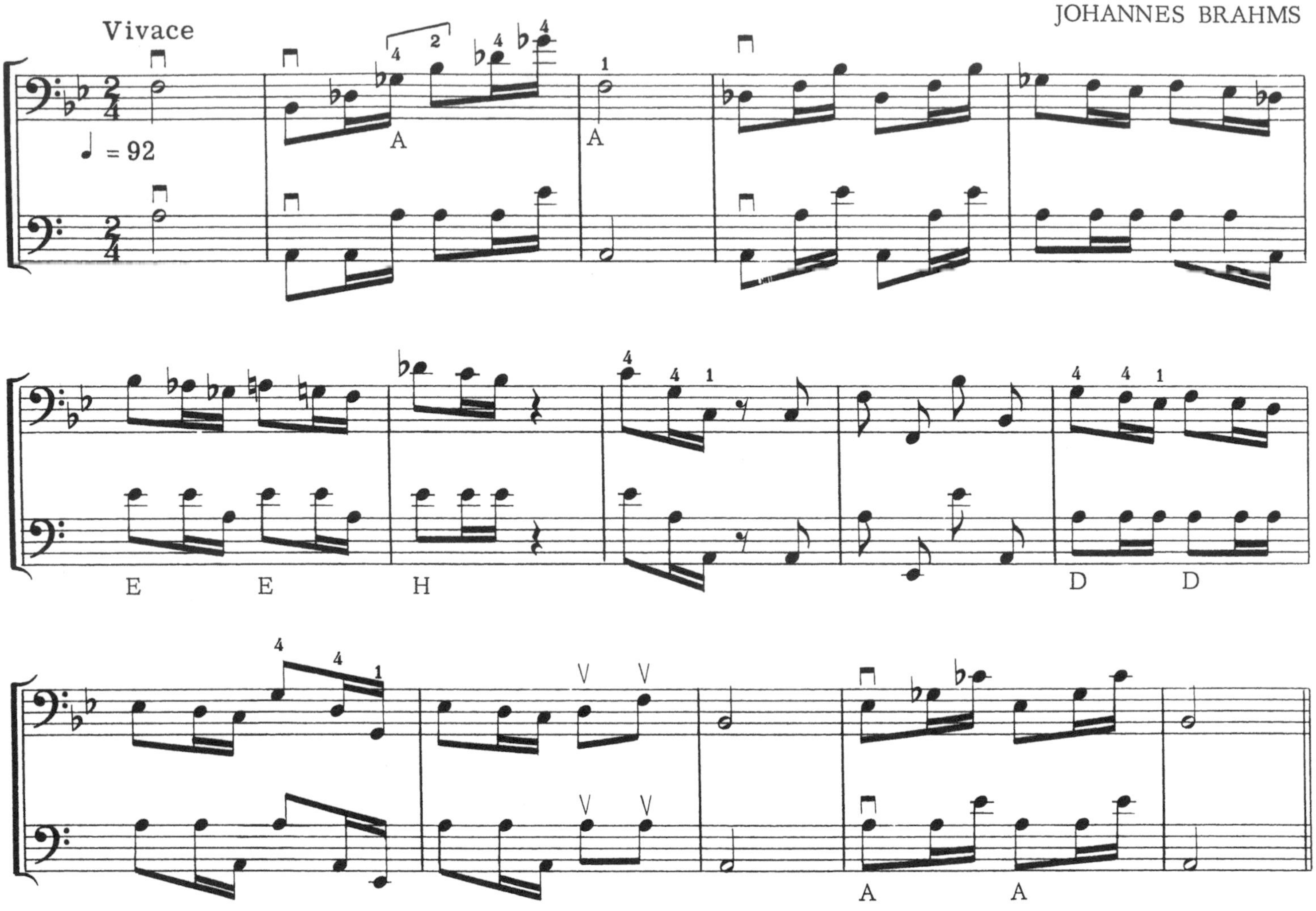

Vivace
♩ = 92
A
A
E
E
H
D
D
A
A

OVERTURE "LEONORE No. 3"

LUDWIG van BEETHOVEN

Allegro (in two)
𝅗𝅥 = 132
D
G
H
E
G
G
F
G

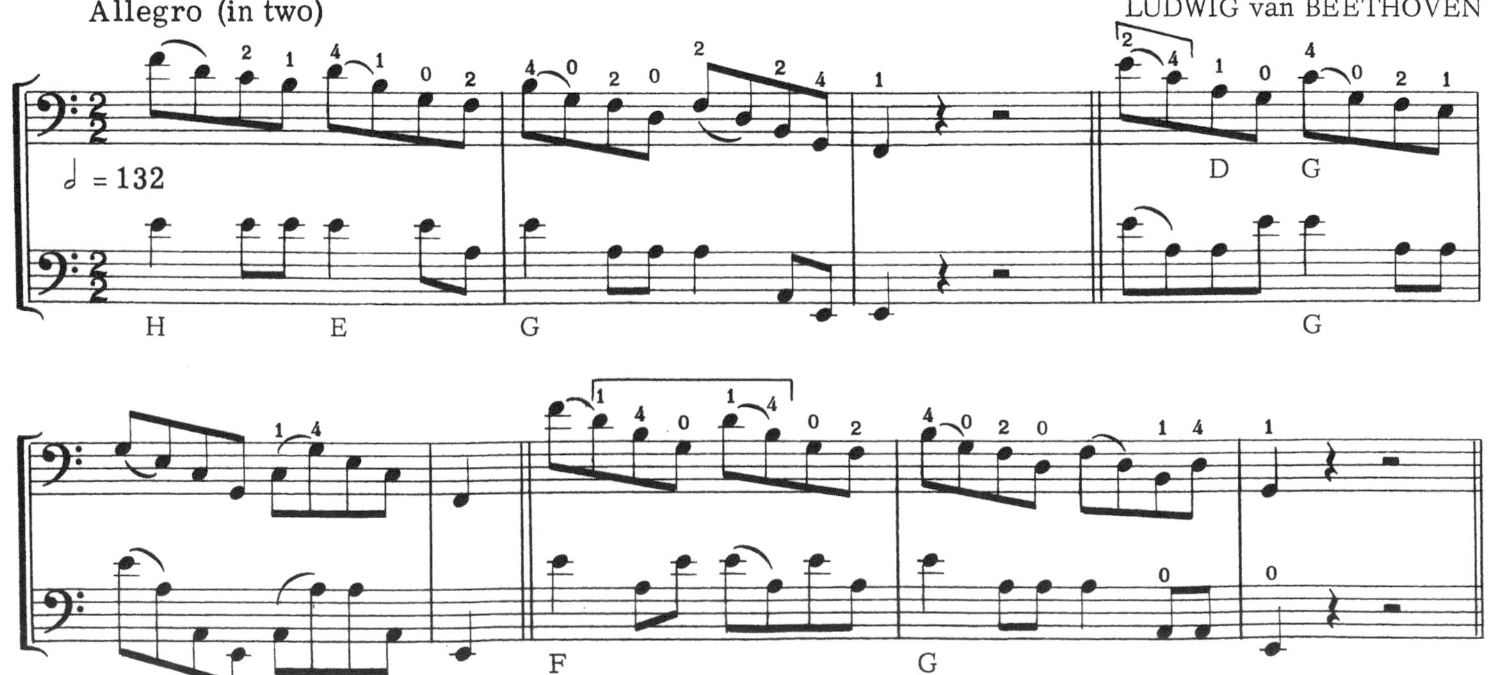

SYMPHONY No. 102

JOSEPH HAYDN

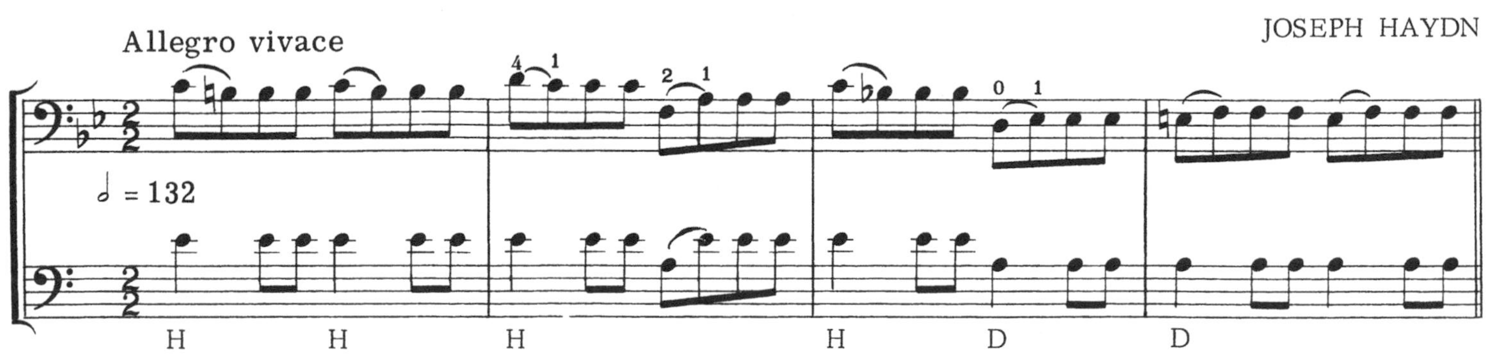

SYMPHONY No. 35

WOLFGANG A. MOZART

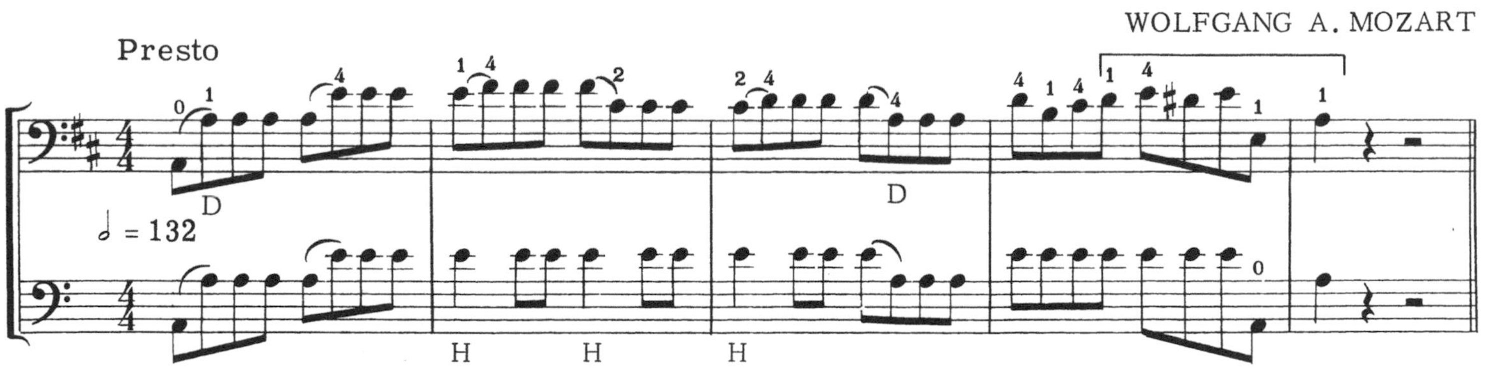

OVERTURE to "DER FREISCHÜTZ"

CARL MARIA von WEBER

SYMPHONY No. 3

FELIX MENDELSSOHN

OVERTURE TO ROMEO AND JULIET

PETER I. TCHAIKOVSKY

Allegro giusto

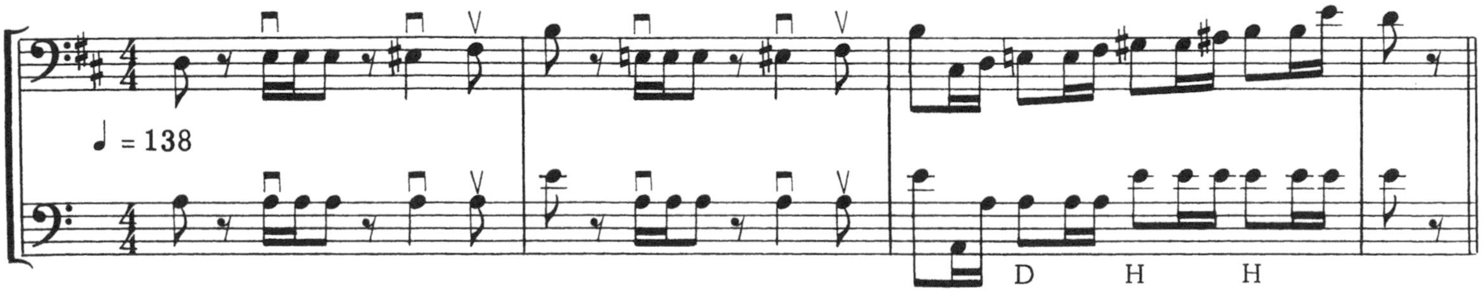

♩ = 138

D H H

C G

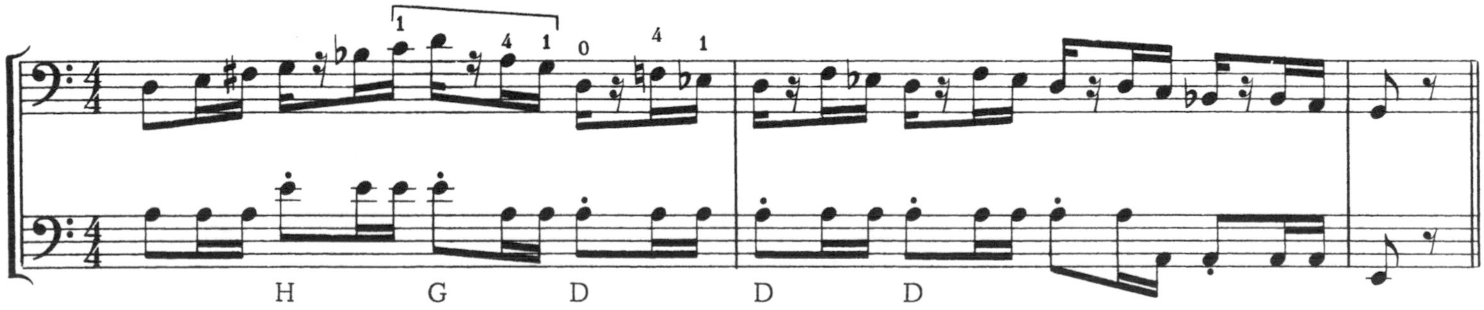

H G D D D

SYMPHONY No. 88

SUITE No. 2 in B MINOR

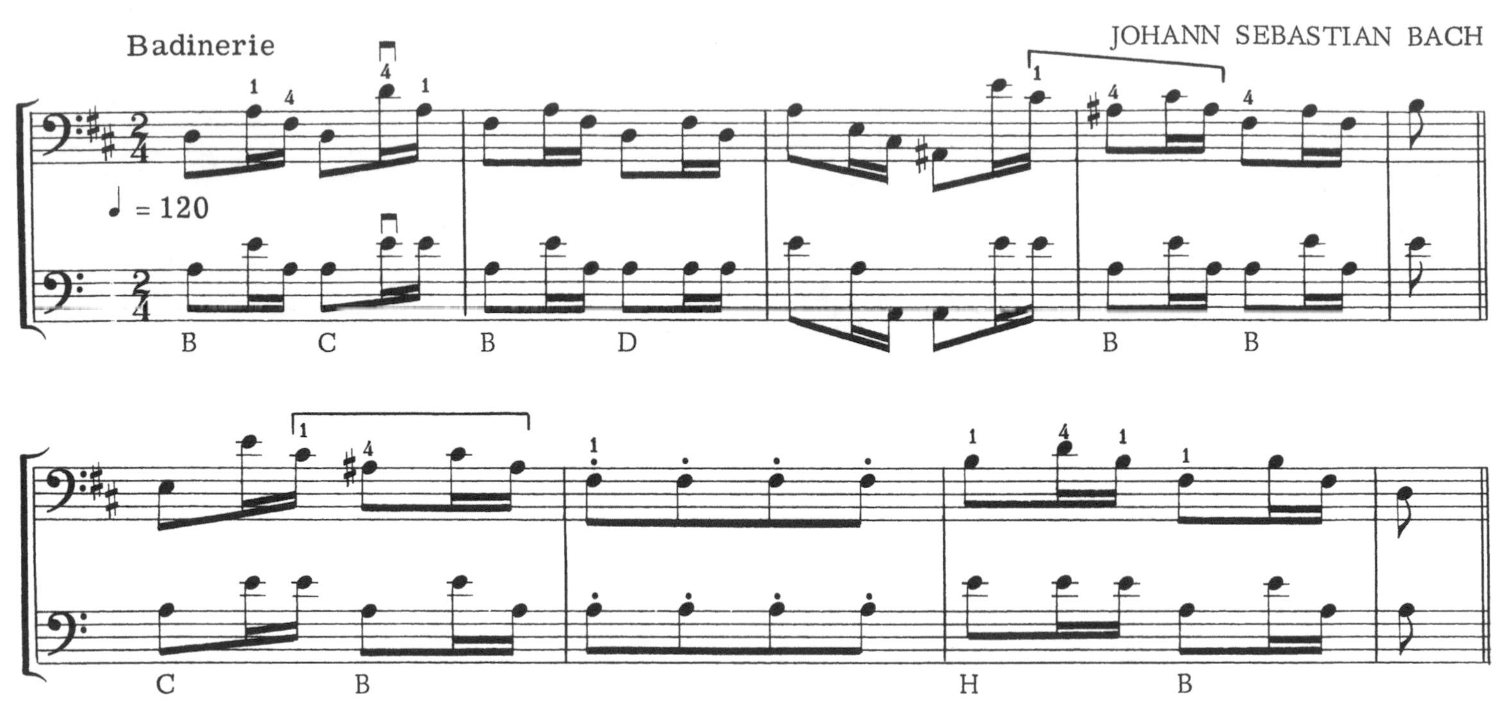

SONATA No. 3

Allegro (sostenuto)

ANTONIO VIVALDI

♩ =104 *f*

H1 H1 D1 D1

H1 D1 D1 D D

C1 C1 C1 C1

♪=72
f
A B C1 D1 E F1 G1 a
B C D E F G b

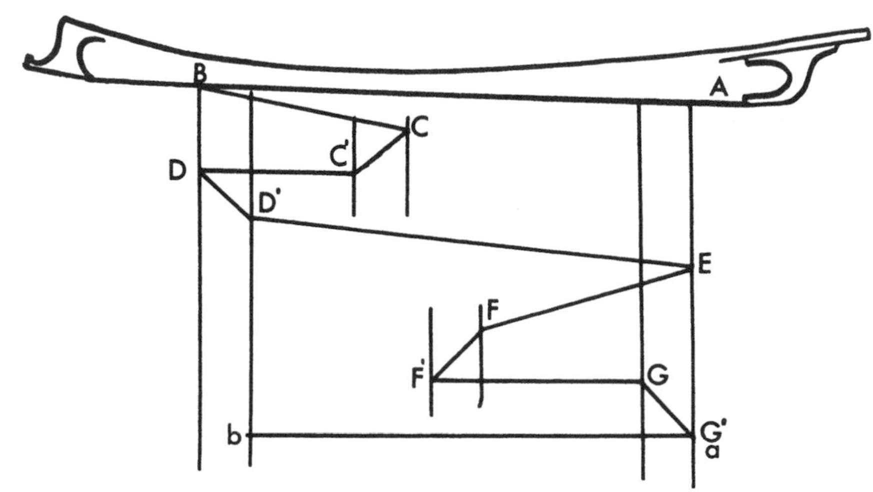
B
A
C
C'
D
D'
E
F
F'
G
b
G'
a

♪=72
f
A B1 C1 D E1 F1 Ga
B C D E F G b

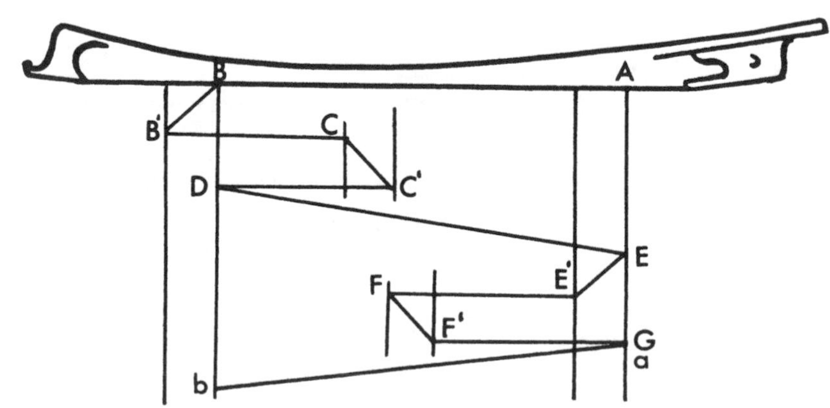
B
A
B'
C
D
C'
E
E'
F
F'
G
a
b

♪=72
f
A B¹ C D¹ E¹ F G¹a
B C D E F G b

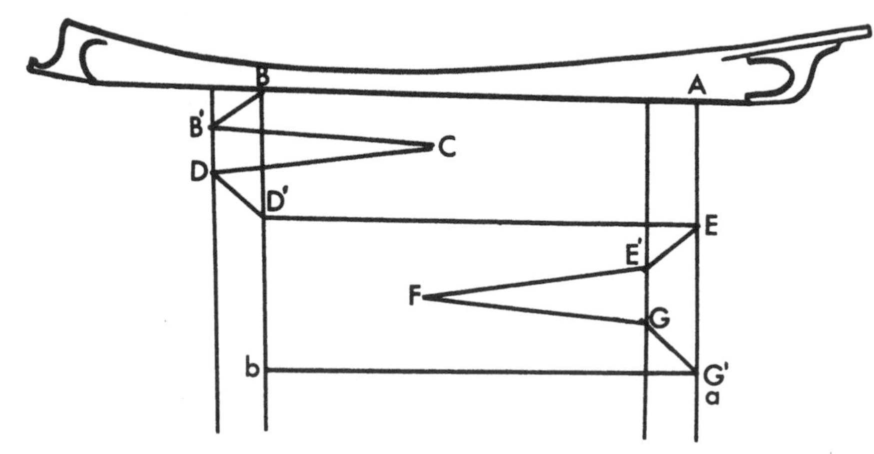
B
A
B'
C
D
D'
E
E'
F
G
b
G'
a

♪=72
f
A B C D E F Ga
B C D E F G b

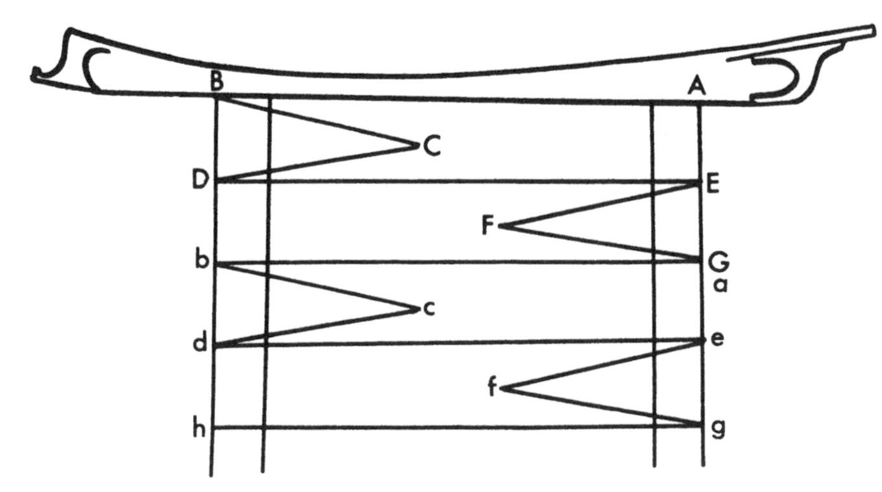
B
A
C
D
E
F
b
G
a
c
d
e
f
h
g

♪=72
f
A B C1 D1 E F1 G1a
B C D E F G b

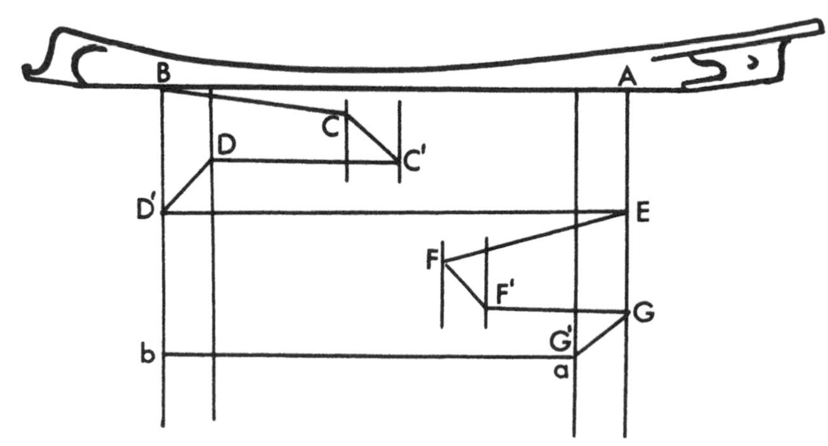
B
A
C
D
C'
D'
E
F
F'
G
G'
b
a

♪=72
f
A B1 C1 D E1 F1 Ga
B C D E F G b

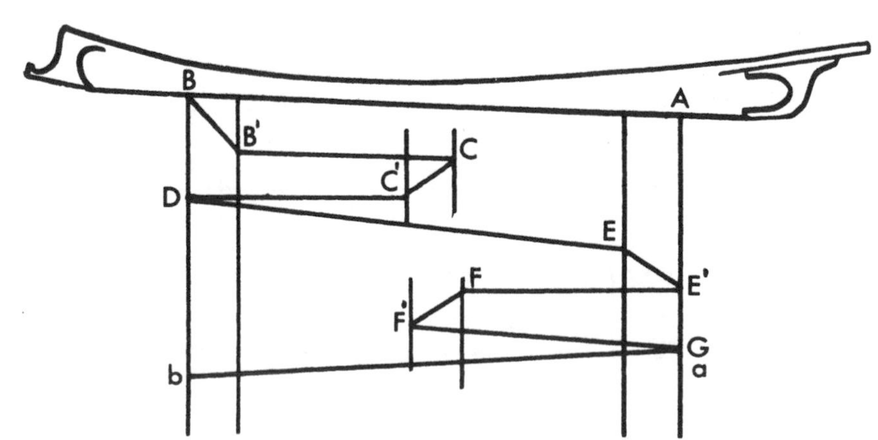
B
A
B'
C
C'
D
E
E'
F
F'
G
a
b

= 72
f
A B1 C D1 E1 F G1 a
B C D E F G b

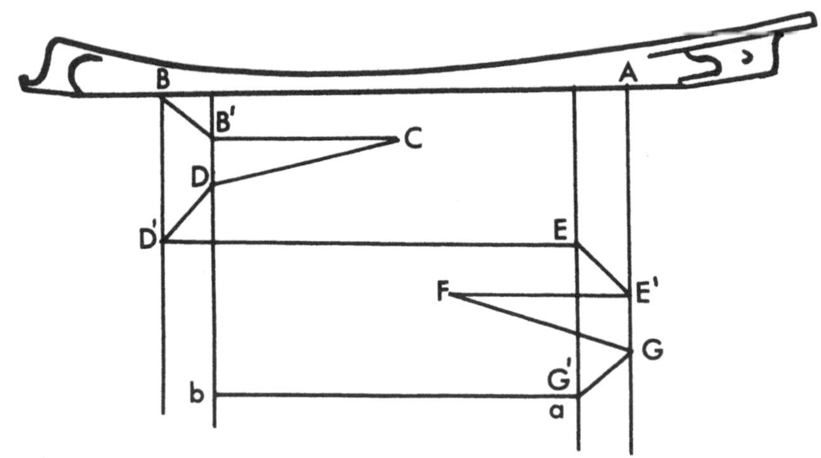

B
A
B'
C
D
D'
E
E'
F
G
G'
a
b

=72
f
A B C D E F Ga
B C D E F G b

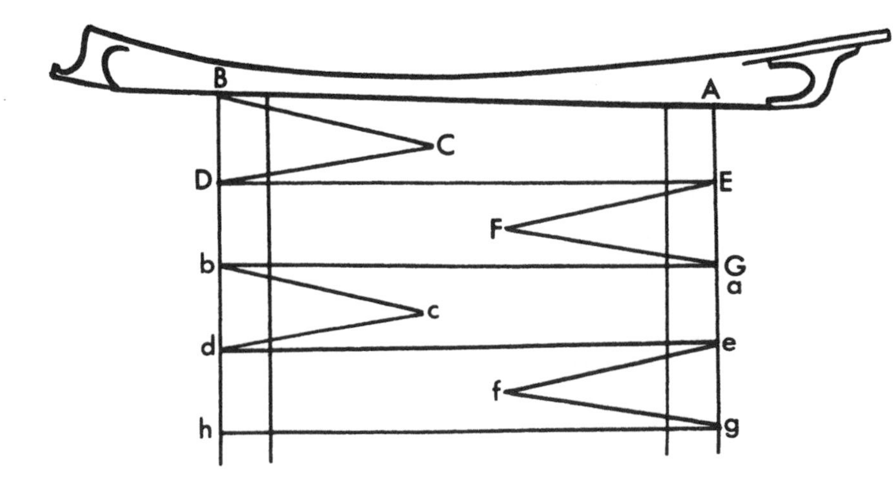

B
A
C
D
E
F
b
G
a
c
d
e
f
h
g

♪ = 72
f
A B C1 D1 E F1 G1a
B C D E F G b

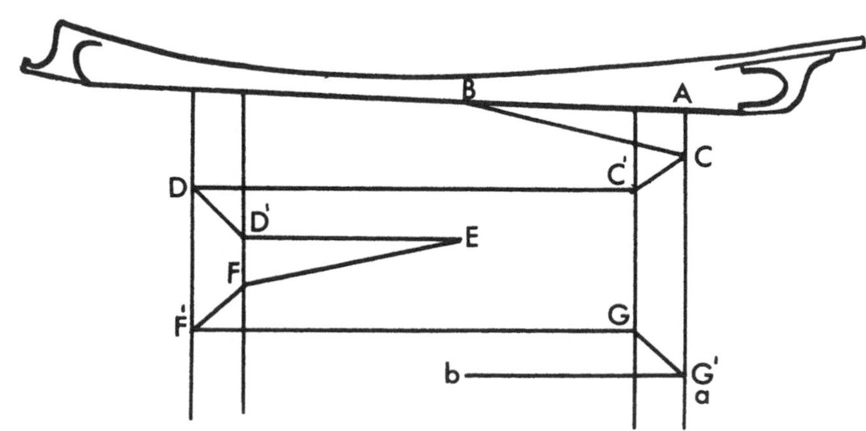
B
A
C
C'
D
D'
E
F
F'
G
b
G'
a

♪ = 72
f
A B1 C1 D E1 F1 Ga
B C D E F G b

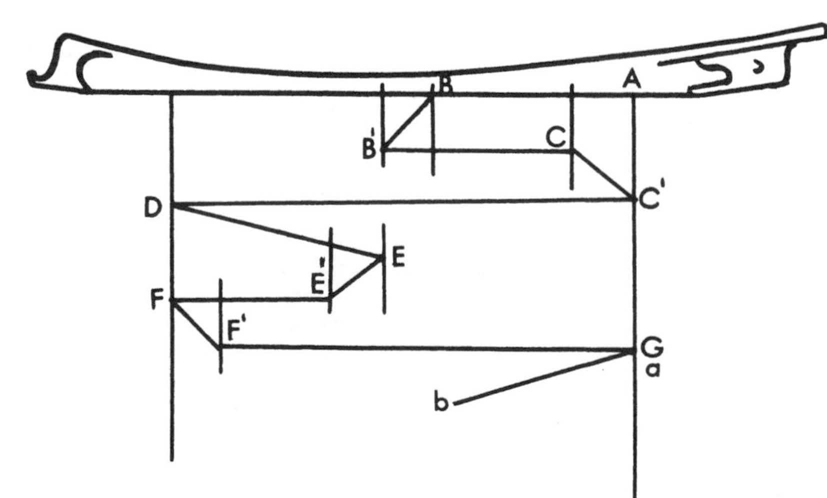
B
A
B'
C
D
C'
E
E'
F
F'
G
a
b

♪ = 72
f
A B¹ C D¹ E¹ F G¹ a
B C D E F G b

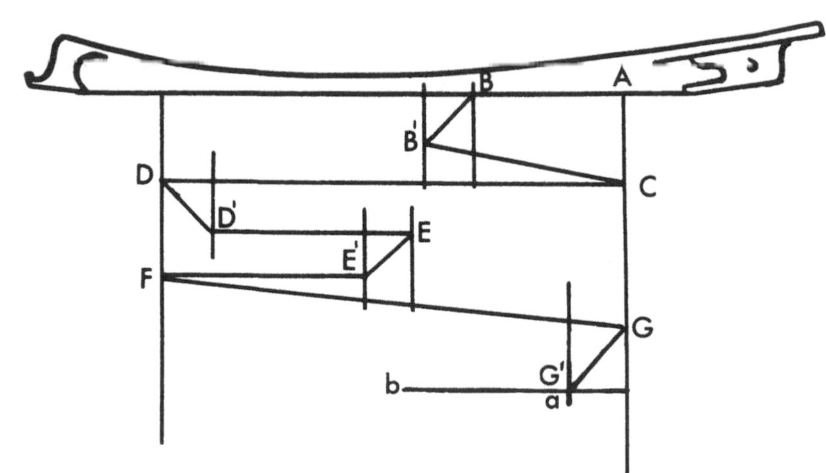
B
A
B'
D
C
D'
E
E'
F
G
G'
b
a

♪ = 72
f
A B C D E F G a
B C D E F G b

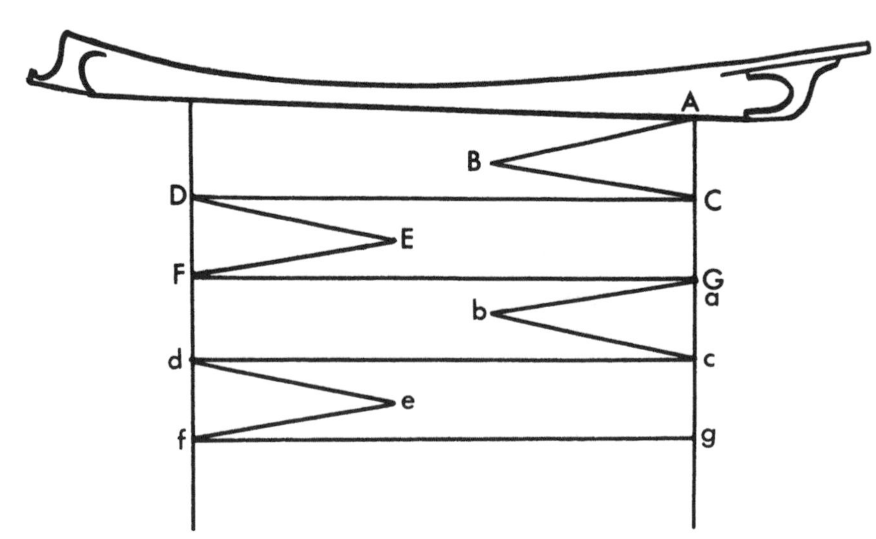
A
B
D
C
E
F
G
a
b
d
c
e
f
g

= 72
A B C1 D1 E F1 G1 a
B C D E F G b

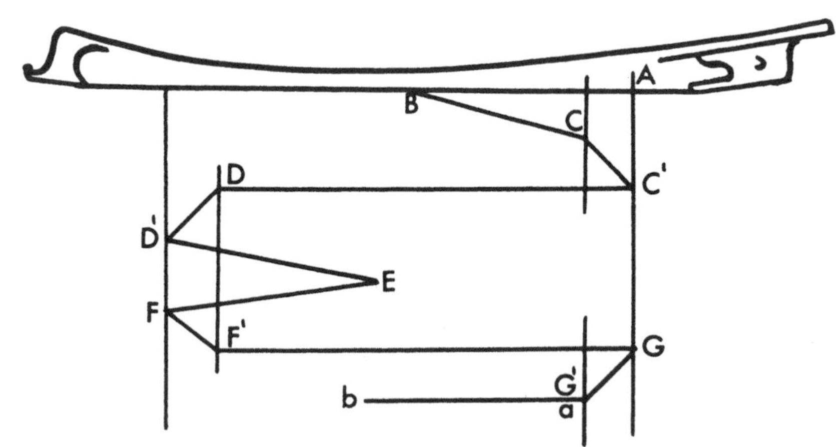
A
B
C
C'
D
D'
E
F
F'
G
G'
a
b

= 72
A B1 C1 D E1 F1 G a
B C D E F G b

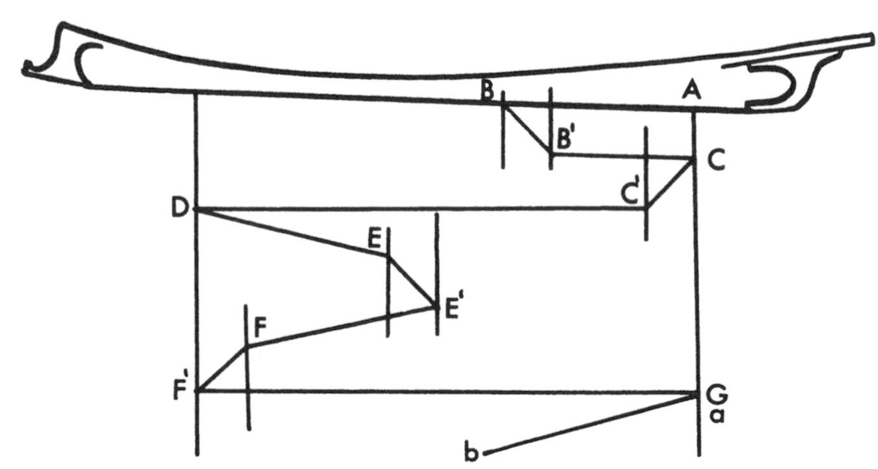
B
A
B'
C
C'
D
E
E'
F
F'
G
a
b

= 72
f
A B1 C D1 E1 F G1a
B C D E F G b

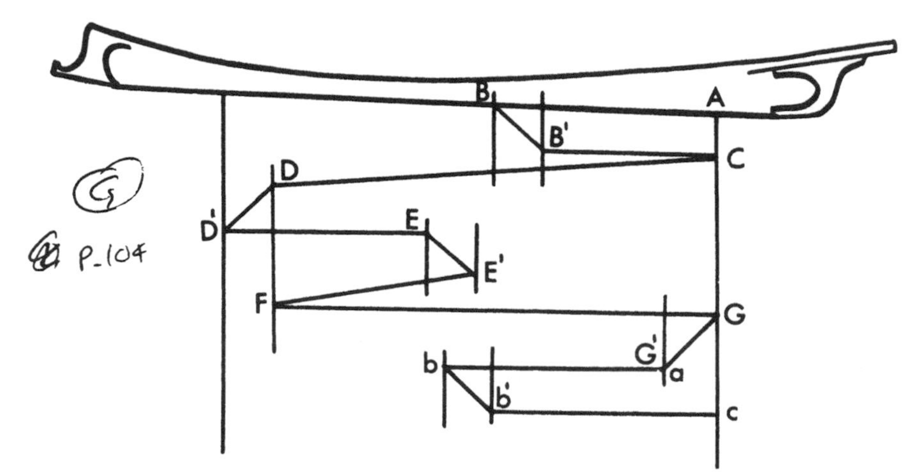
B
A
B'
C
D
D'
E
E'
F
G
G'
a
b
b'
c

SECTION IV

PATTERN I

Suggested procedure for practice: Each pattern is played first at a metronome marking of ♩ = 90. The tempo is accelerated until ♩ = 176, with the bow on the string *(Détaché)*. With the metronome set at ♩ = 192, the patterns are practiced with a *Spiccato* bowing. At 𝅗𝅥. = 88 the bow remains again on the string.

ETUDES

PATTERN I

Allegro giusto ♩ = 168

This exercise is to be practiced with a *Martelé* bowing; each note beginning with a sharp attack and separated from the next note.

Moderato ♩ = 144

BOWINGS

PATTERN I

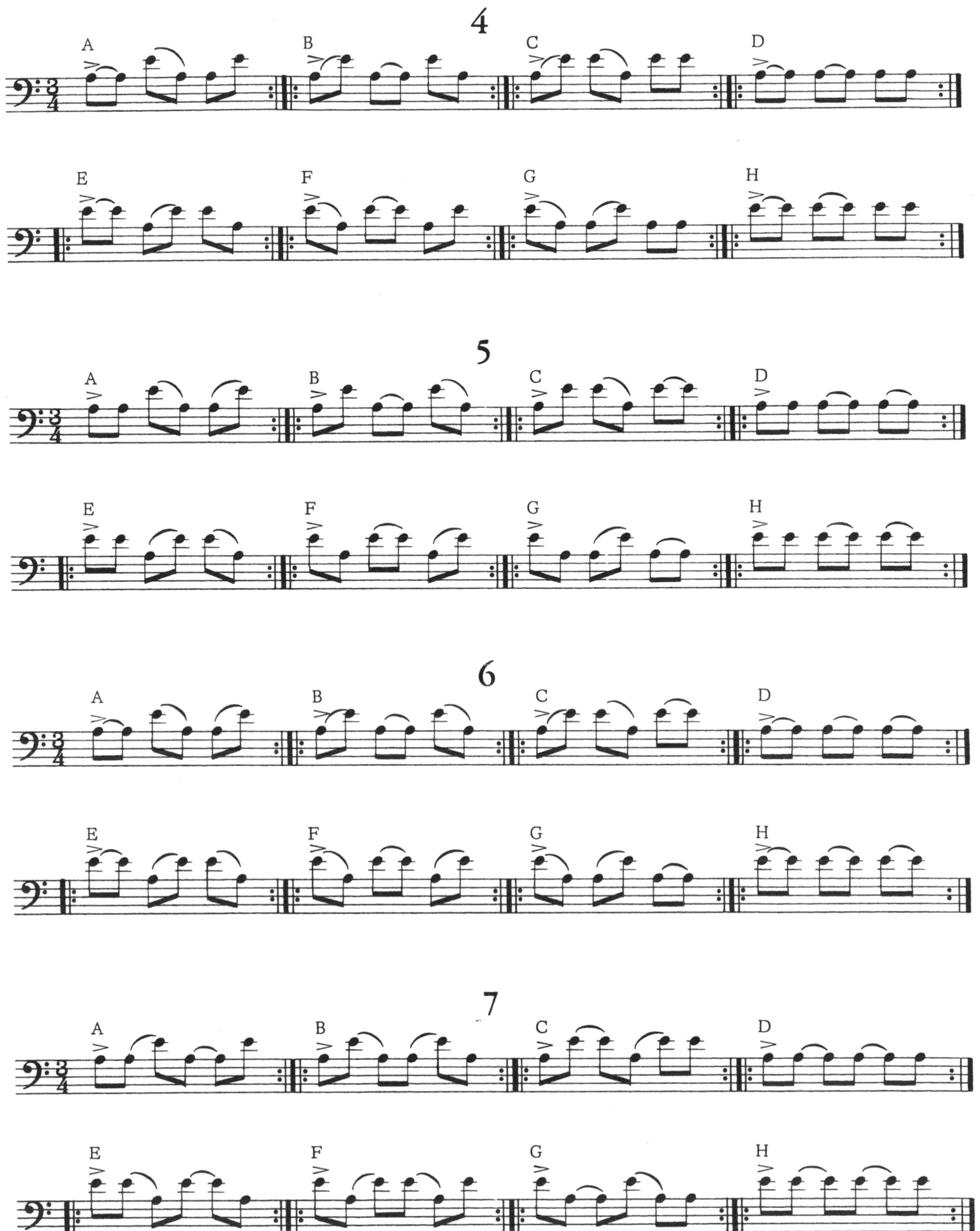
4
A
B
C
D
E
F
G
H
5
A
B
C
D
E
F
G
H
6
A
B
C
D
E
F
G
H
7
A
B
C
D
E
F
G
H

ETUDES

BOWINGS (PATTERN I)

PERMUTATIONS OF PATTERN I

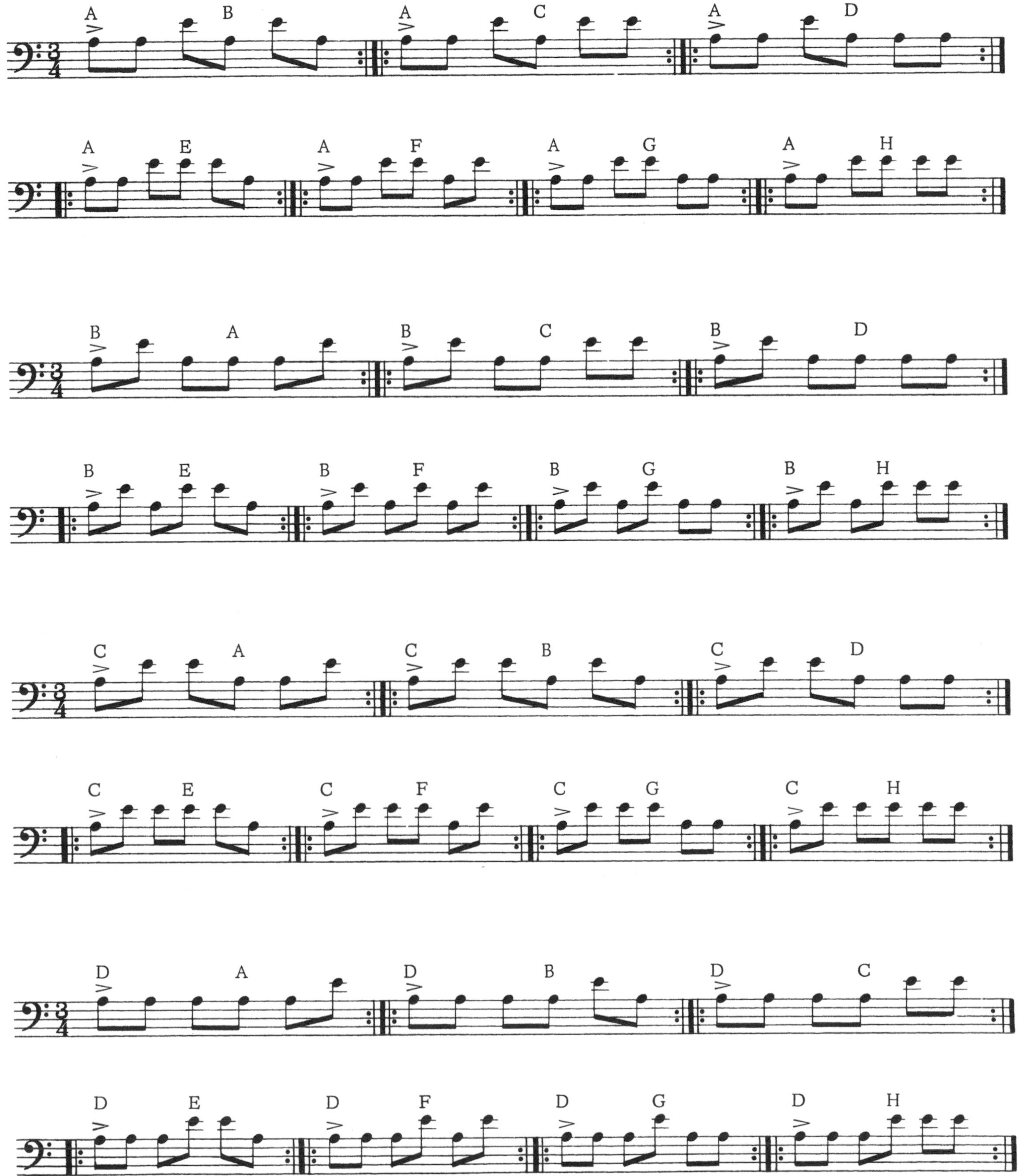

E A
E B
E C
E D
E F
E G
E H
F A
F B
F C
F D
F E
F G
F H
G A
G B
G C
G D
G E
G F
G H
H A
H B
H C
H D
H E
H F
H G

ETUDES

PERMUTATIONS OF PATTERN I

Allegro molto ♩ = 152 to ♩ = 176 *(spiccato)* to ♩ = 208 *(détaché)*

Allegro molto ♩ = 168 to ♩ = 184 *(spiccato)*

BOWINGS

PERMUTATIONS OF PATTERN I

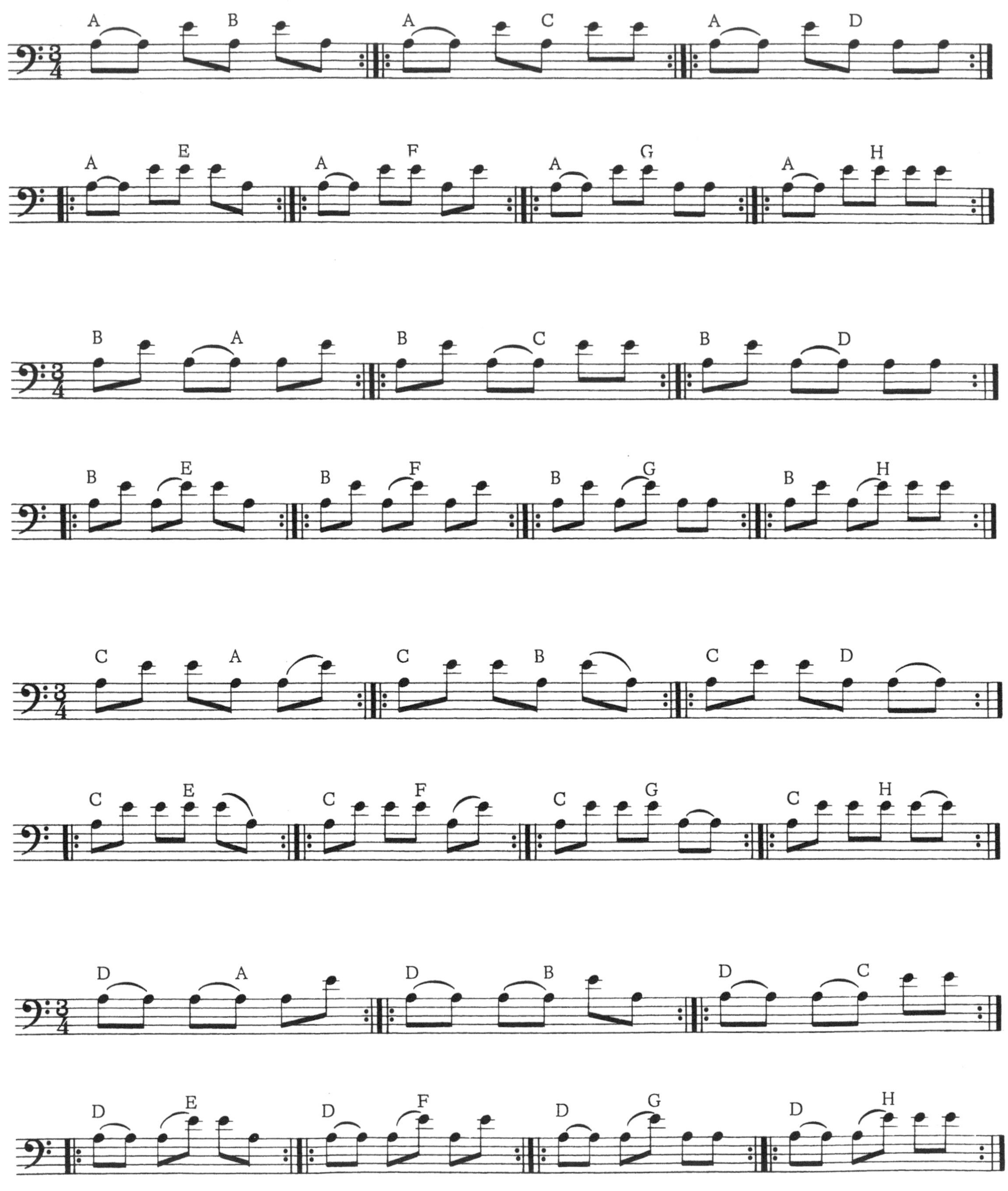

E
A
E
B
E
C
E
D
E
F
E
G
E
H
F
A
F
B
F
C
F
D
F
E
F
G
F
H
G
A
G
B
G
C
G
D
G
E
G
F
G
H
H
A
H
B
H
C
H
D
H
E
H
F
H
G

ETUDES

BOWINGS (PERMUTATIONS OF PATTERN I)

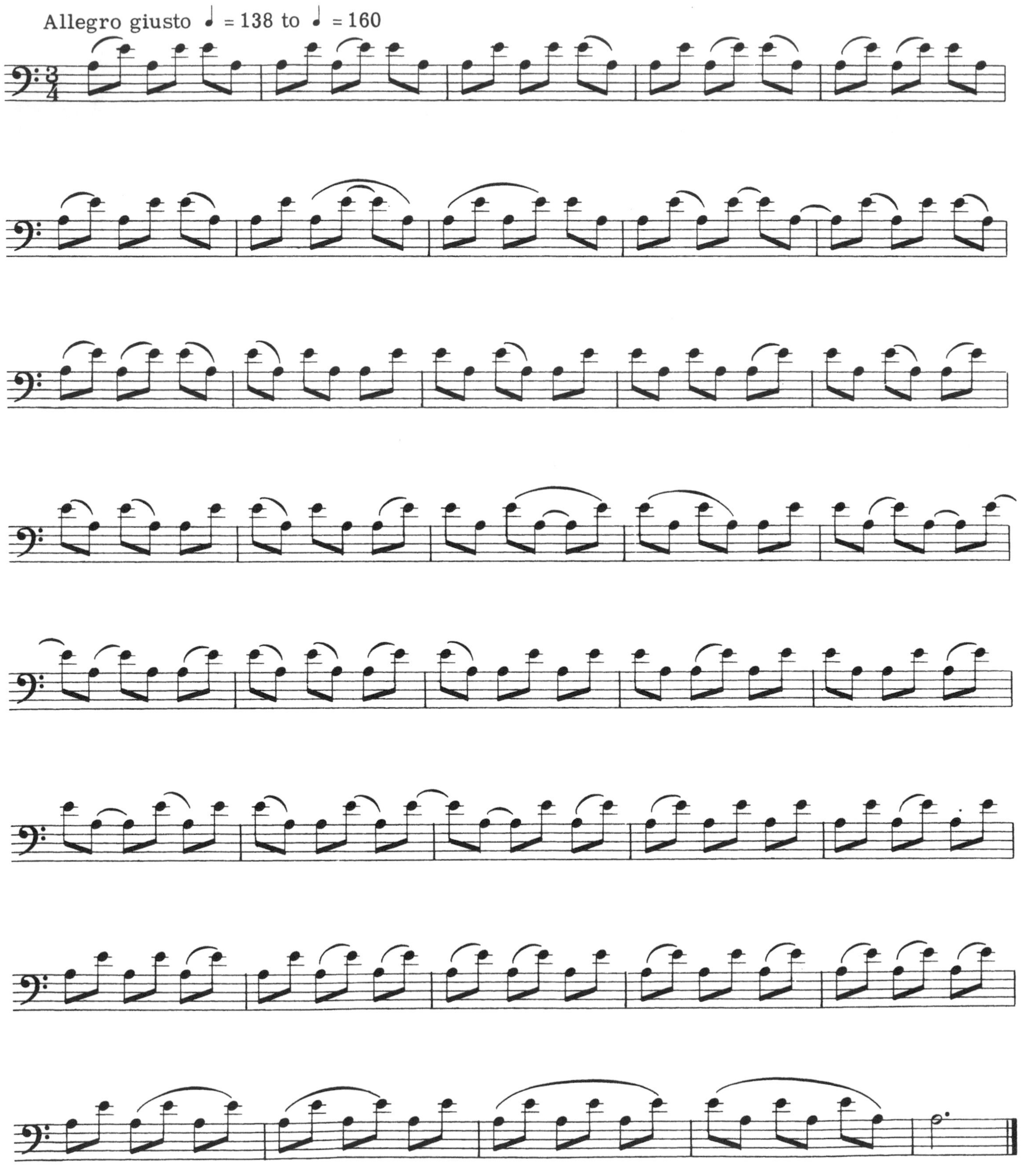

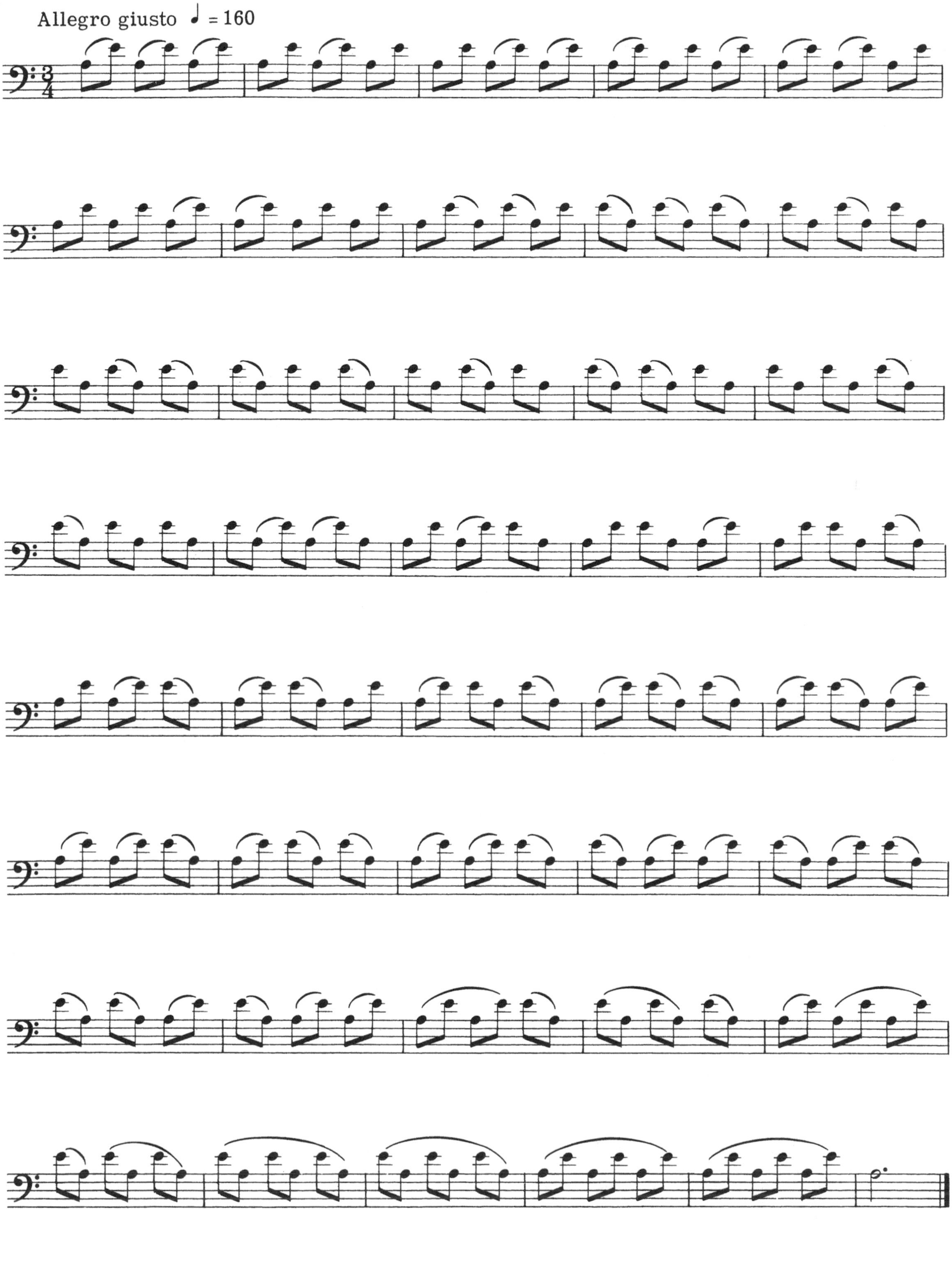

Allegro giusto ♩ = 160

Allegro giusto ♩ = 138 to ♩ = 160

SYMPHONY No. 1

JEAN SIBELIUS

Scherzo

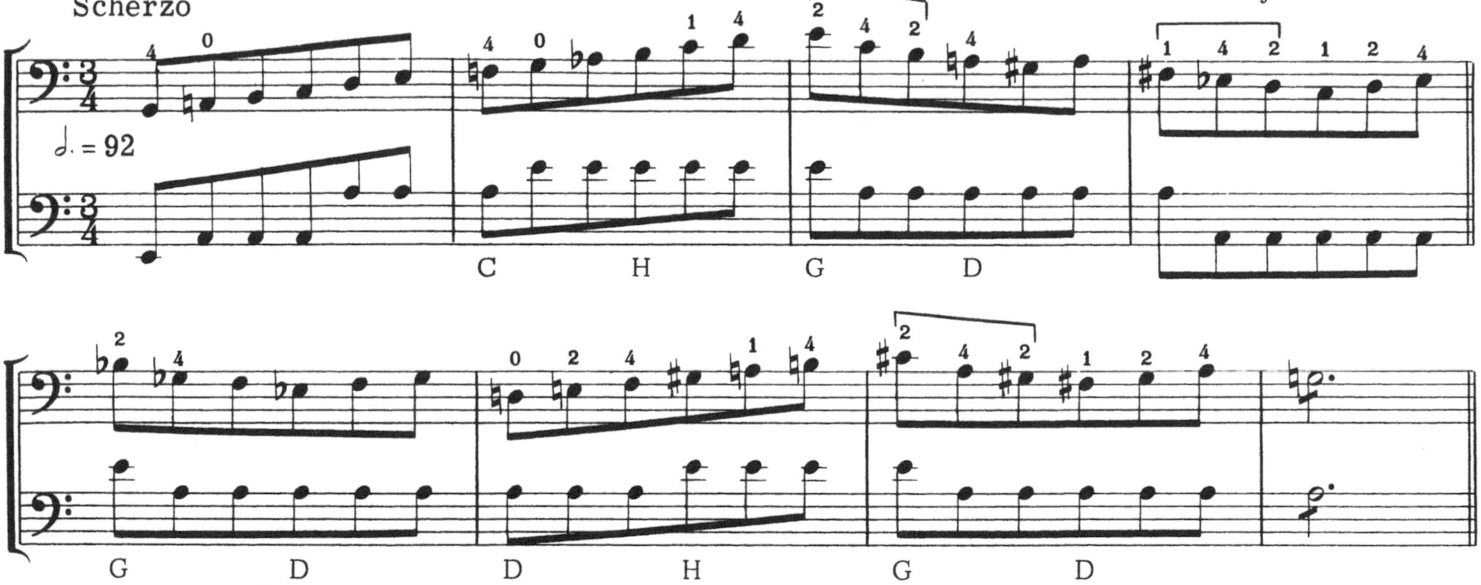

𝅗𝅥. = 92

SONATA

HENRY ECCLES

Vivace (in one)

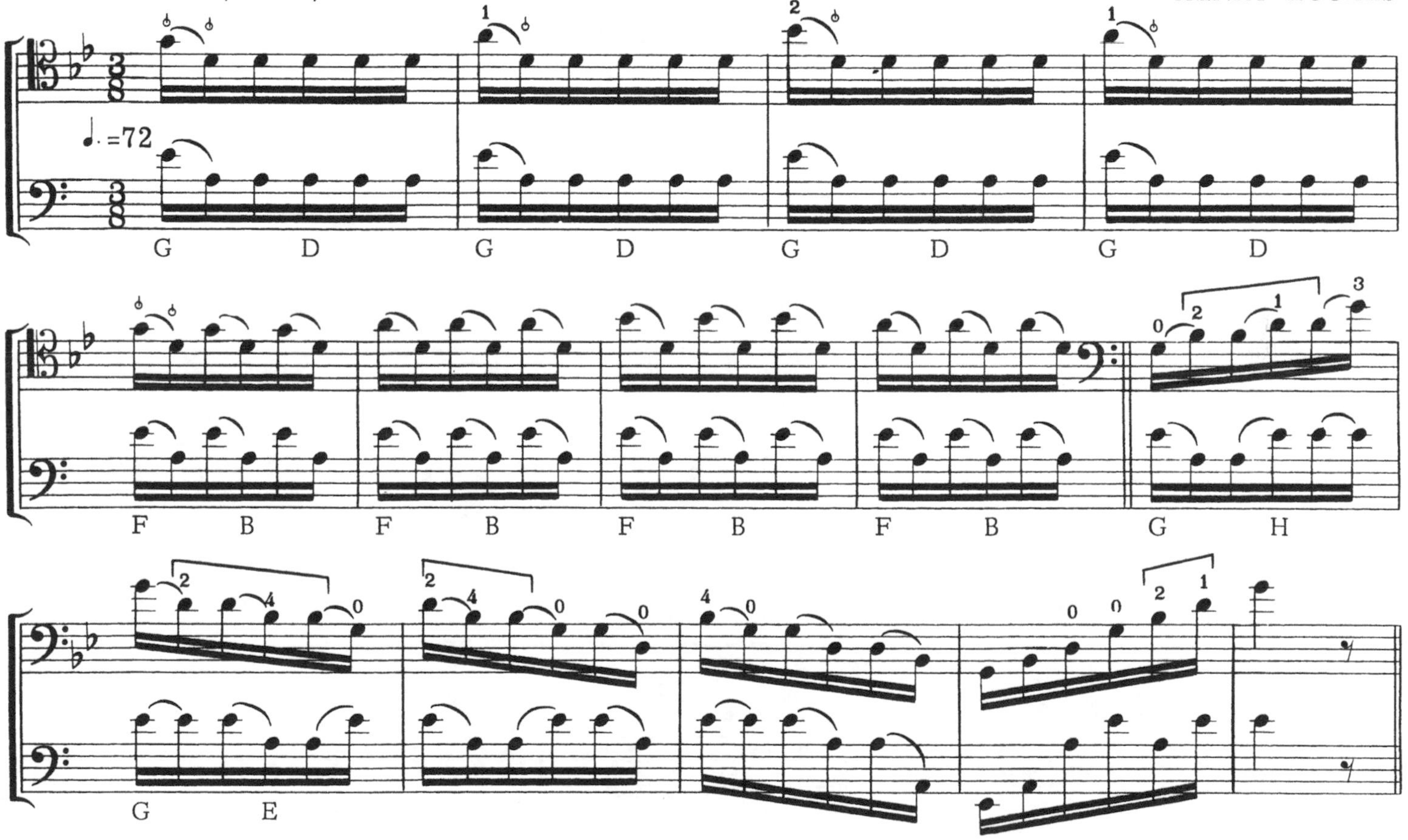

♩. = 72

SYMPHONY No. 8

LUDWIG van BEETHOVEN

Allegro vivace

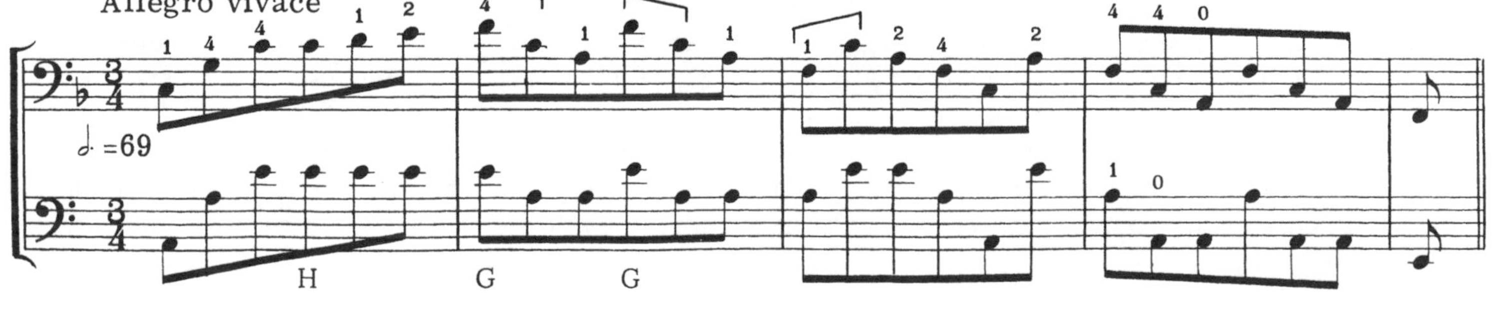

𝅗𝅥. = 69

SONATA No. 5

ANTONIO VIVALDI

SCYTHIAN SUITE

SERGEI PROKOFIEFF

SYMPHONY No. 39

WOLFGANG A. MOZART

Allegro

♩ =160

E F F G

E F D

E G D A

* As illustrated above, a change in fingerings will often induce a change in the bowing patterns. In analyzing the change of patterns one can readily observe, as in the measure indicated by an asterisk, that what is often judged to be an ideal fingering ("ideal" judged by the fact that all the notes of the measure can be played in one position) induces, however, a pattern that presents a complex bowing problem; whereas, in making a move or moves out of position, or even in preferring an open string, very often will induce a sequence of patterns whose similarity and familiarity will afford the passages to be played with greater fluidity.

SYMPHONY No. 9

LUDWIG van BEETHOVEN

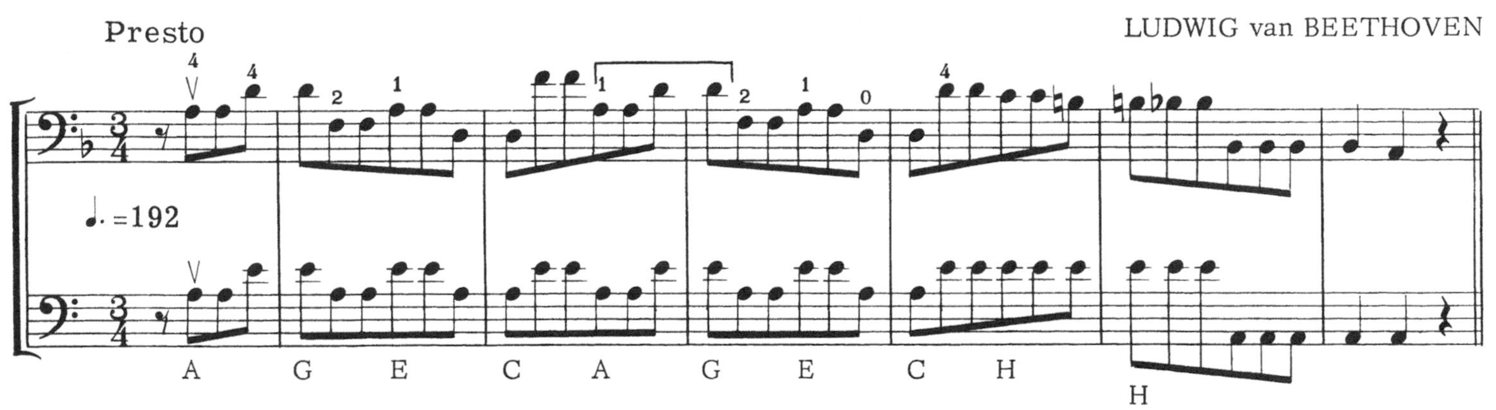

CONCERTO

Rondo Sostenuto

E. D. STEIN

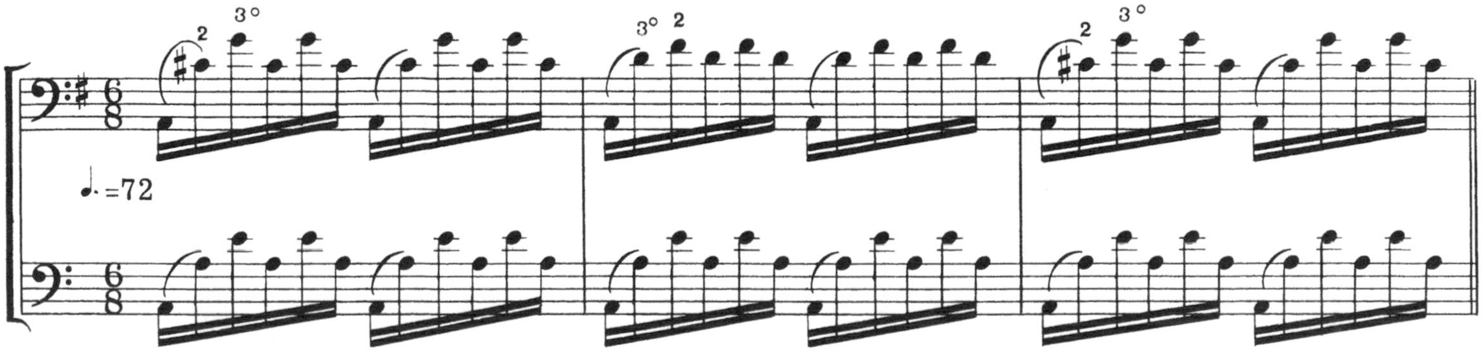

♩. = 72

Più mosso

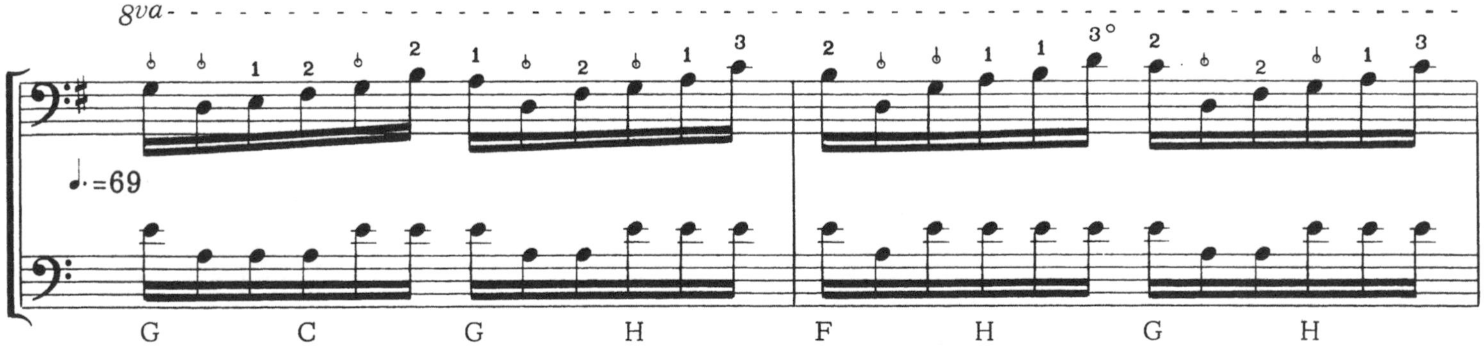

8va

♩. = 69

G C G H F H G H

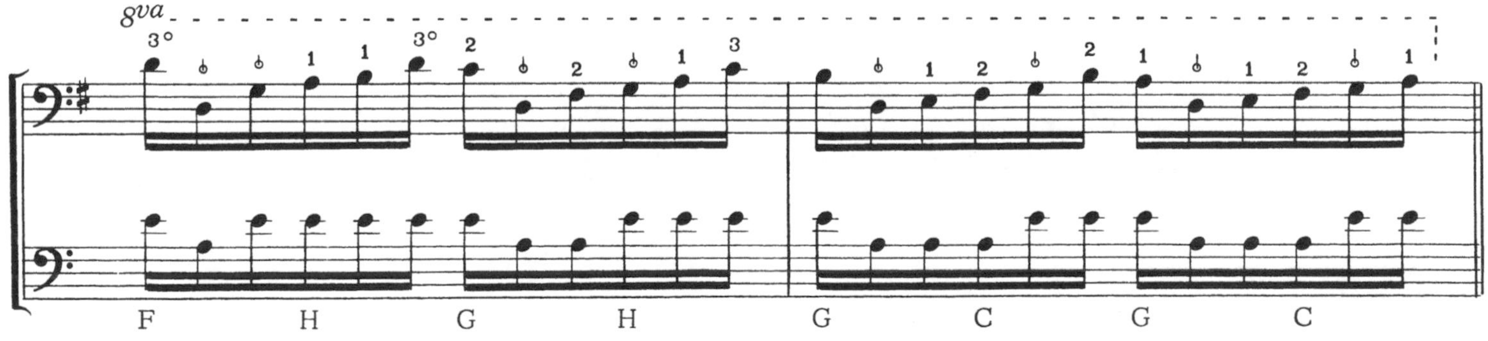

8va

F H G H G C G C

SYMPHONY No. 45 ("Farewell")

Allegro assai

JOSEPH HAYDN

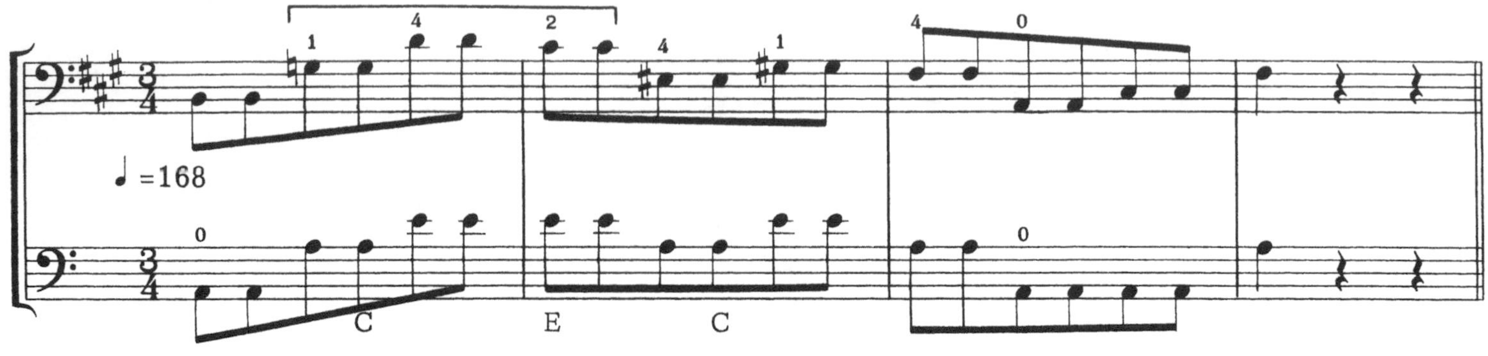

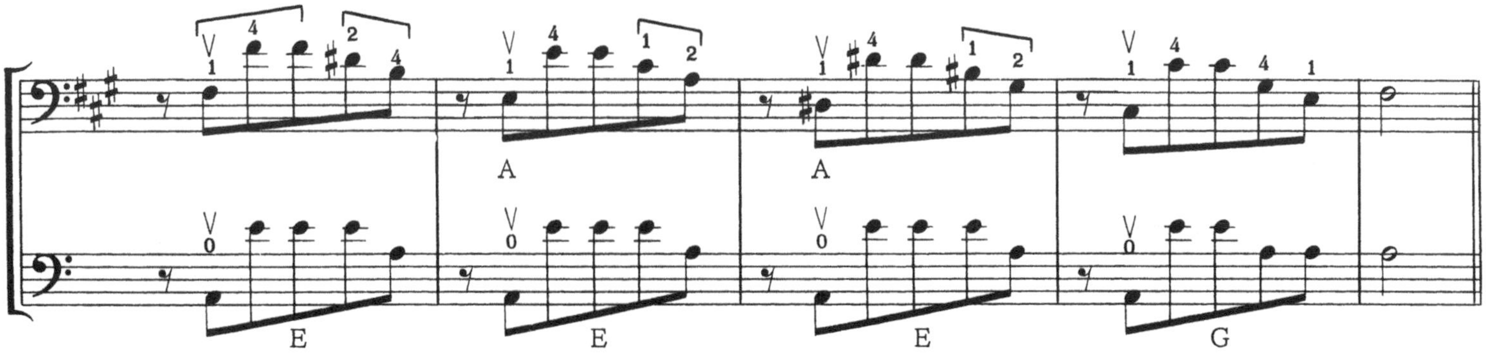

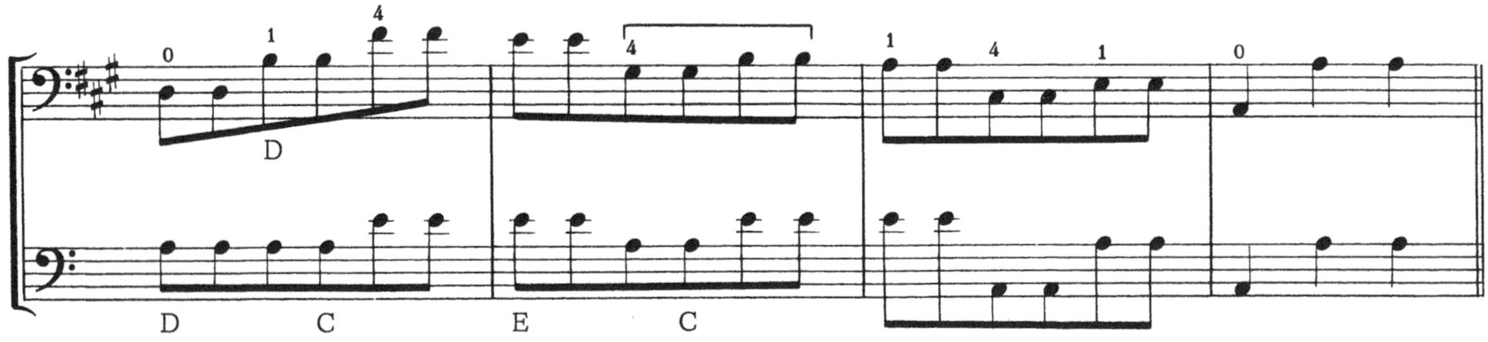

♩ = 168

SYMPHONY No. 2

JOHANNES BRAHMS

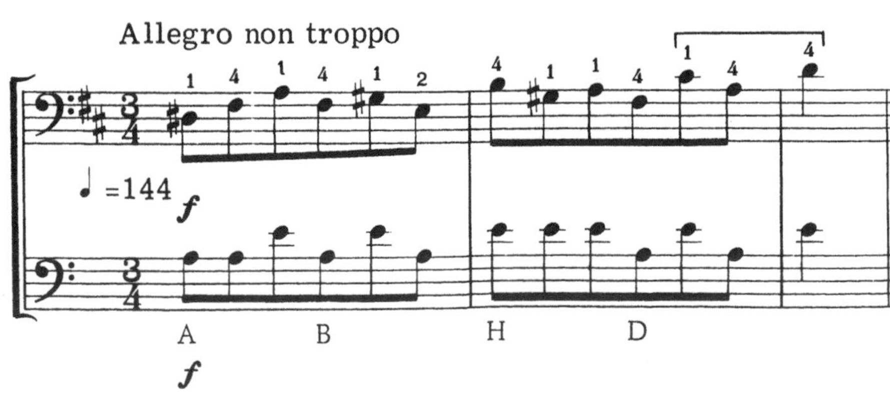

COURANTE from SONATA

Allegro con spirito

HENRY ECCLES

SECTION V

Patterns, Etudes and Excerpts relating to three and four strings

BOWING DRILLS FOR THE UPPER THREE STRINGS

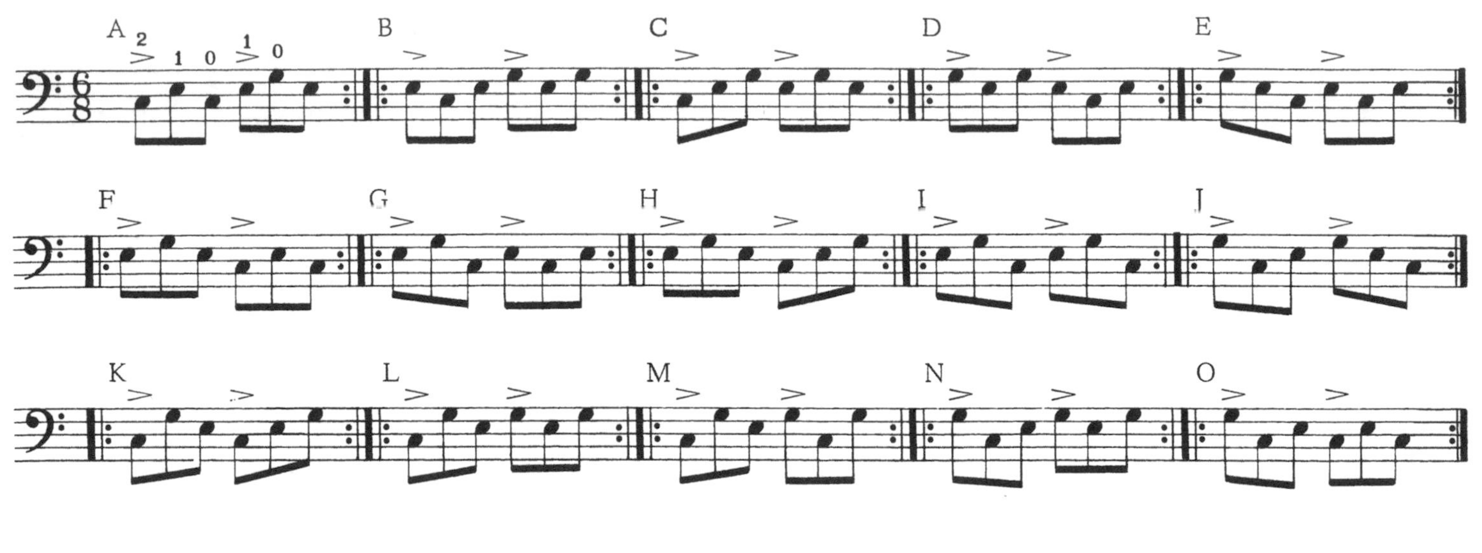

BOWINGS

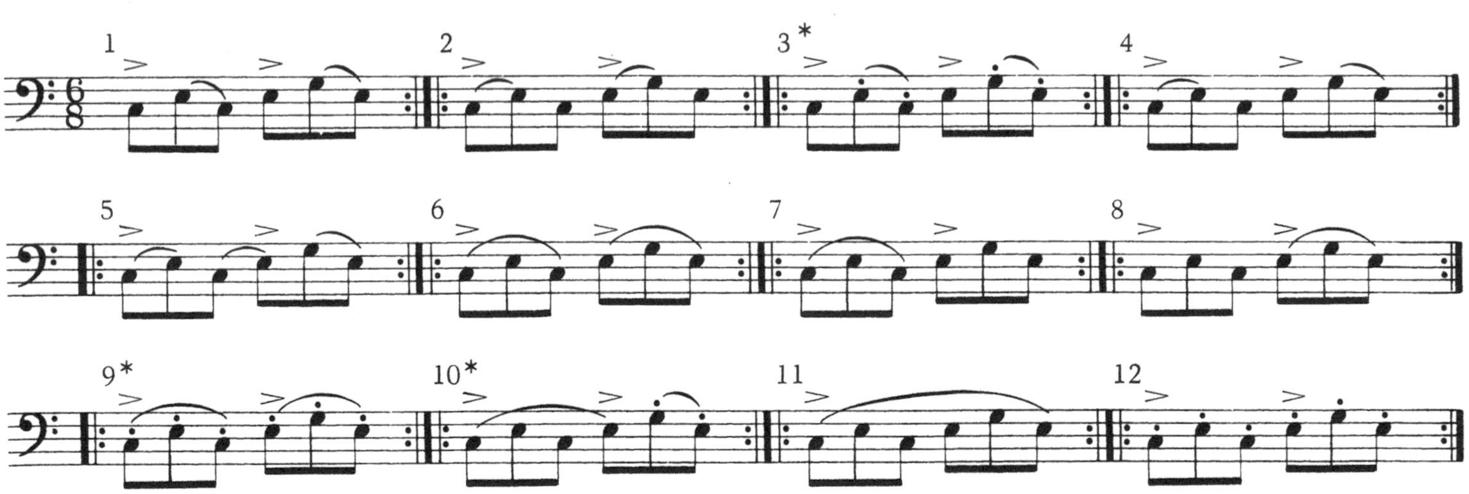

* The dotted notes are to be played alternately on the string *(Staccato)* and off the string *(Flying Spiccato)*.

BOWING DRILLS FOR THE LOWER THREE STRINGS

ETUDE

UPPER THREE STRINGS

ETUDE

BOWINGS FOR THE UPPER THREE STRINGS

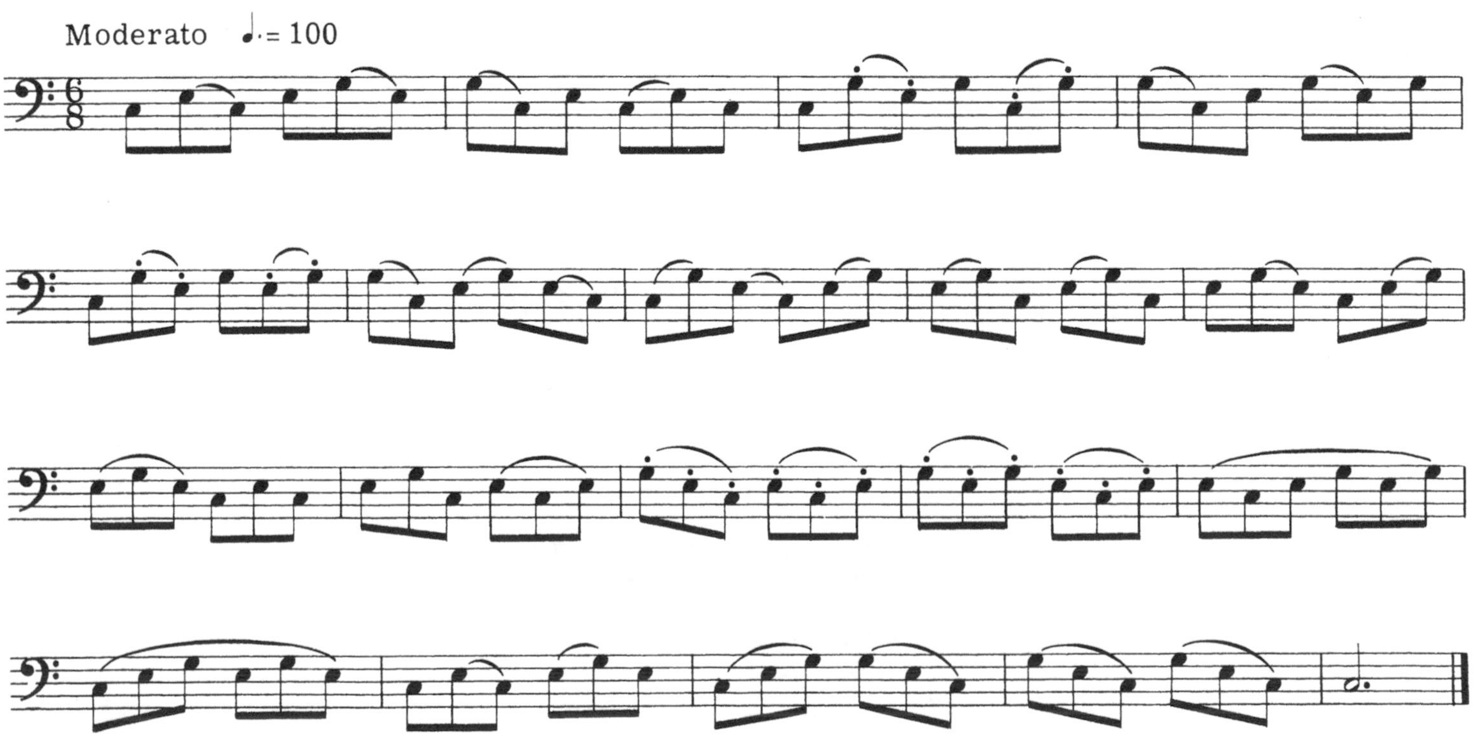

BOWING DRILLS IN THREE QUARTER METER

(UPPER THREE STRINGS)

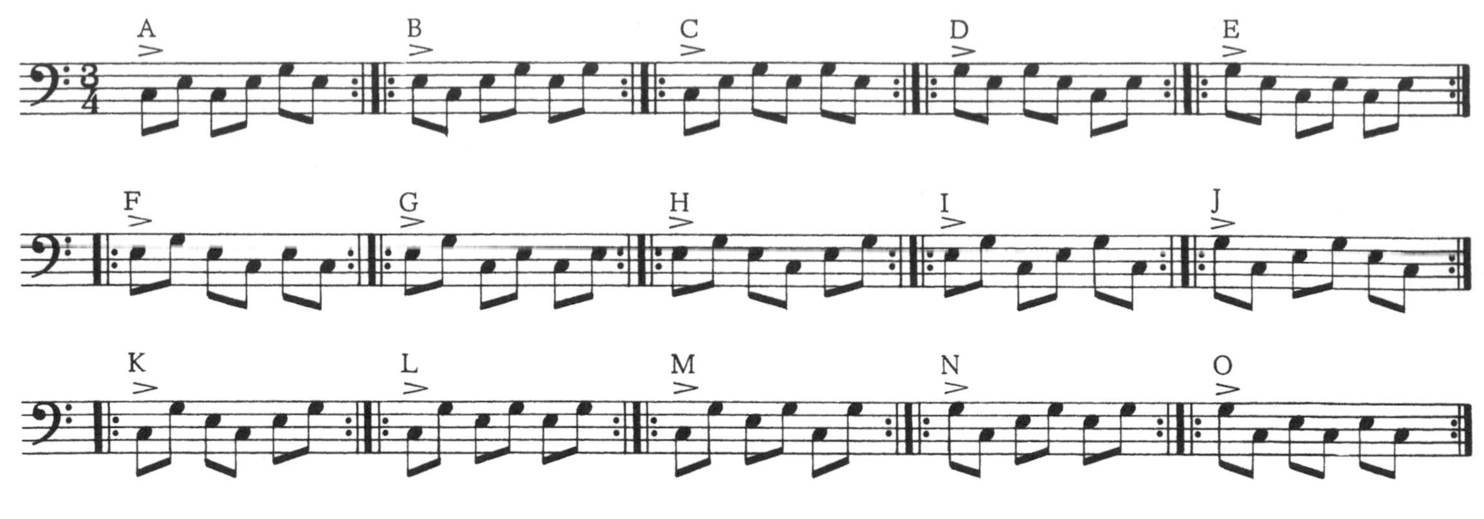

BOWINGS

BOWING DRILLS IN THREE QUARTER METER

(LOWER THREE STRINGS)

ETUDE

IN THREE QUARTER METER - UPPER THREE STRINGS

ETUDE

BOWINGS

SYMPHONY No. 1

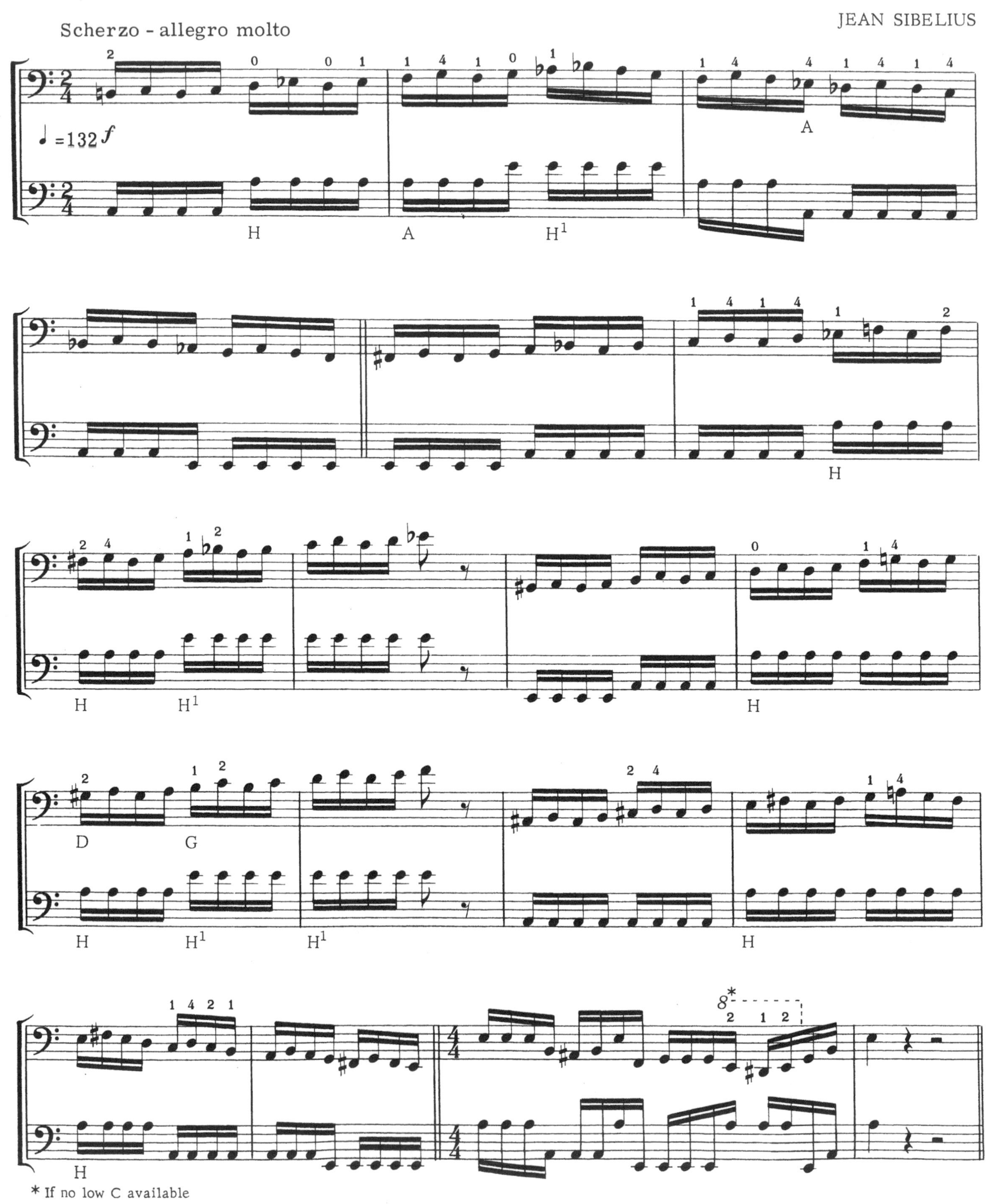

BRANDENBURG CONCERTO No. 2

JOHANN SEBASTIAN BACH

MAGNIFICAT

JOHANN SEBASTIAN BACH

Allegro moderato

♩ =108

OVERTURE "LEONORE No. 3"

LUDWIG van BEETHOVEN

SYMPHONY No. 5

LUDWIG van BEETHOVEN

SONATA No. 2

ANTONIO VIVALDI

Allegro

♩ =108 *mf*

SYMPHONY No. 9

LUDWIG van BEETHOVEN

*Begin the study of this excerpt at the metronome mark 𝅗𝅥 = 112; advance gradually through 𝅗𝅥 = 116, 𝅗𝅥 = 120, 𝅗𝅥 = 126 to the final tempo indication by Beethoven of 𝅗𝅥 = 132.

SECTION VI

BOWING DRILLS FOR THE UPPER TWO STRINGS

VARIATIONS

G
H
I
J

K
L
M
N

Vivo ♩ = 200 *(spiccato)*

0 0 4 0 4 1 0

4 4 4 1 4 1 4

♩ = 200

0 0 4 0

♩ = 200

The dotted notes are to be played alternately on the string *(Staccato)* and off the string *(Flying Spiccato)*.

The dotted notes are to be played alternately on the string *(Staccato)* and off the string *(Flying Spiccato)*.

This bowing *(Piqué)* is to be played in the upper half of the bow; the dotted eighth note short *(Martelé)* and the sixteenth note with a smoother stroke *(Détaché)*.

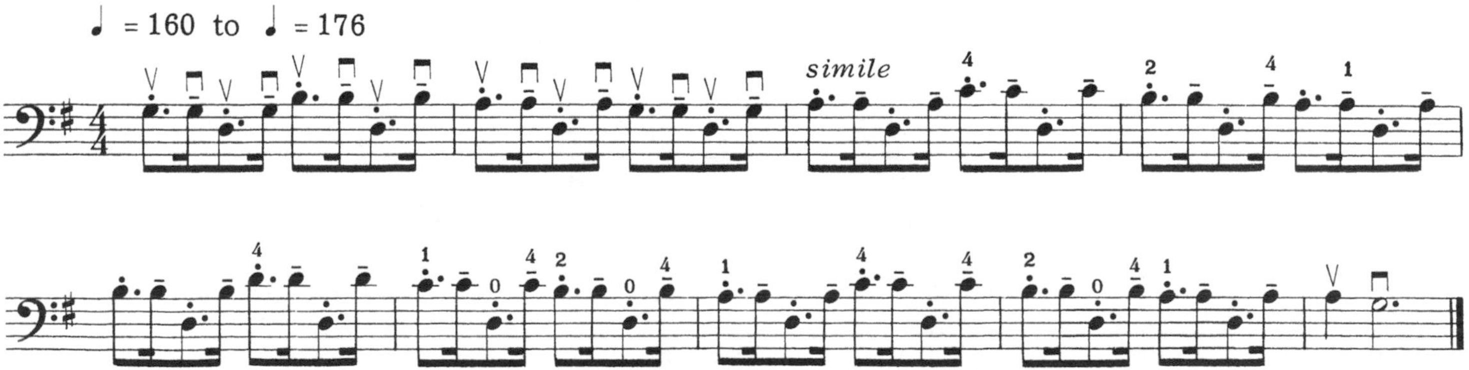

Moderato ♩ = 120

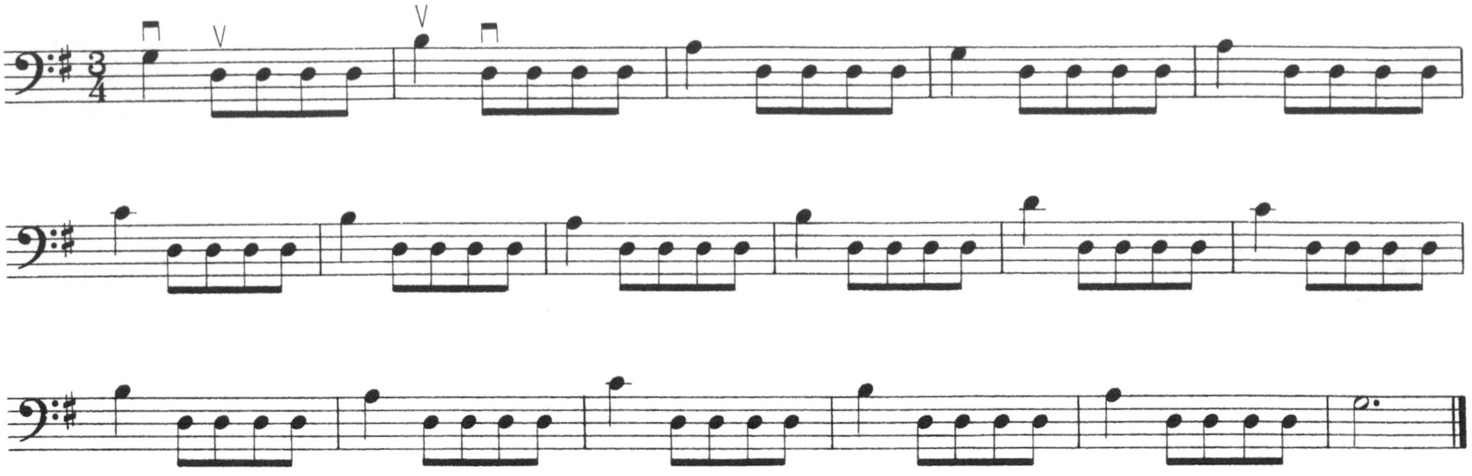

The dotted notes are to be played with a *Flying Spiccato* bowing.

Allegro ♪ = 200

Moderato ♩ = 120 to ♩ = 138

Allegro ♩. = 92

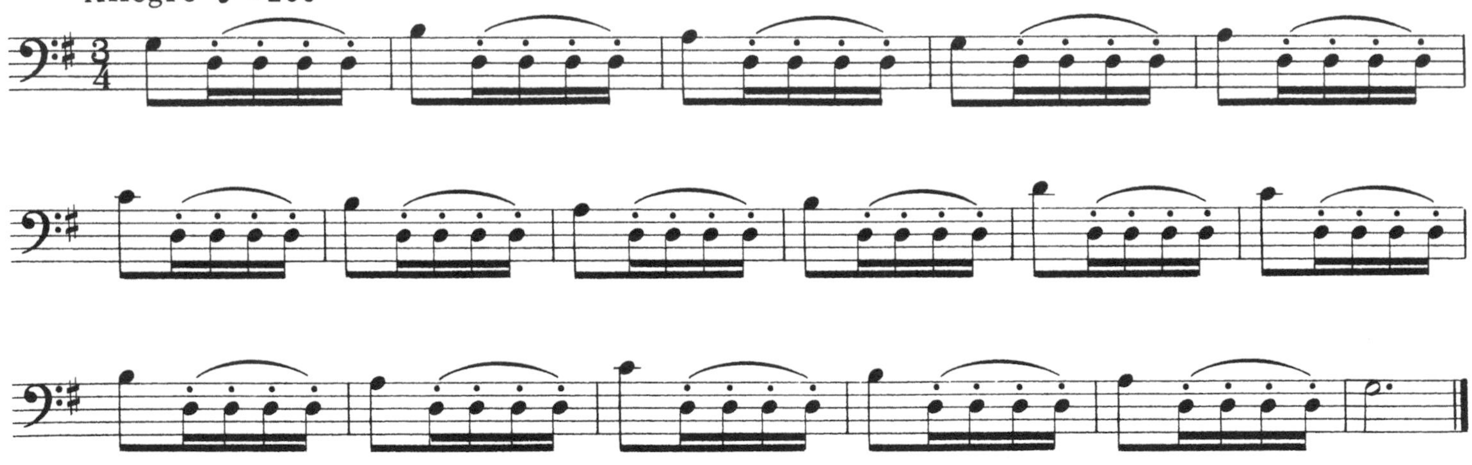

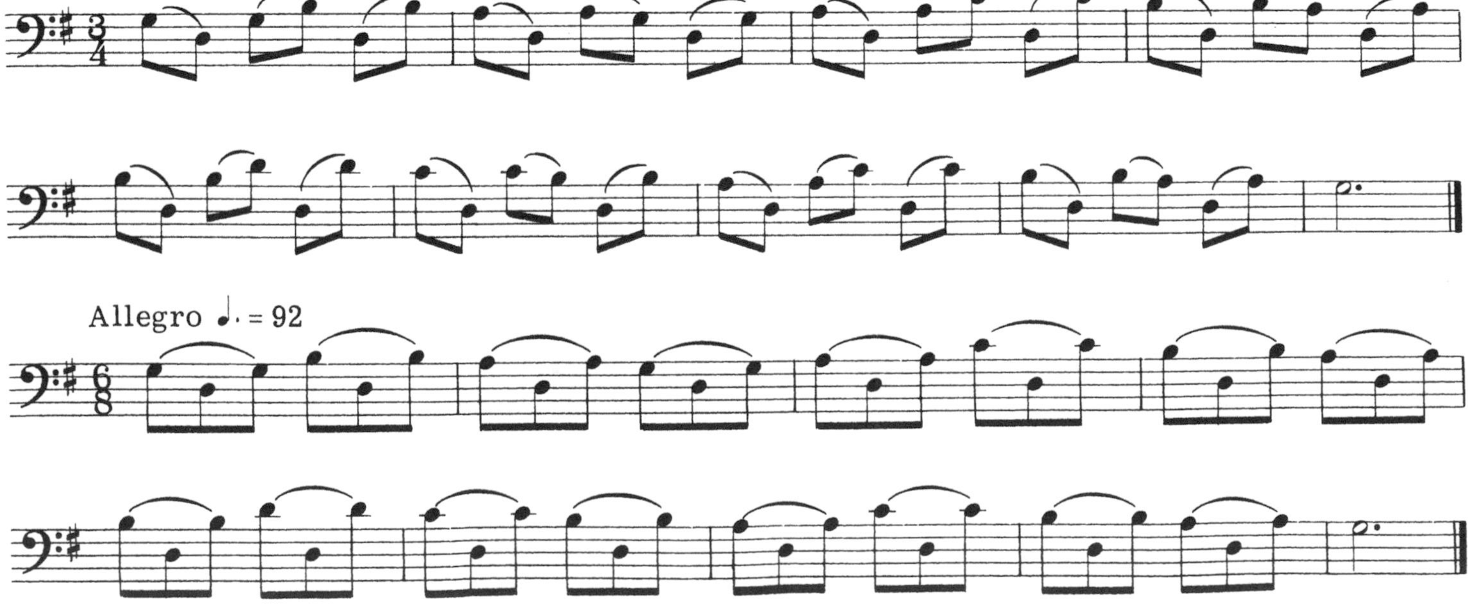

Allegro ♪ = 160

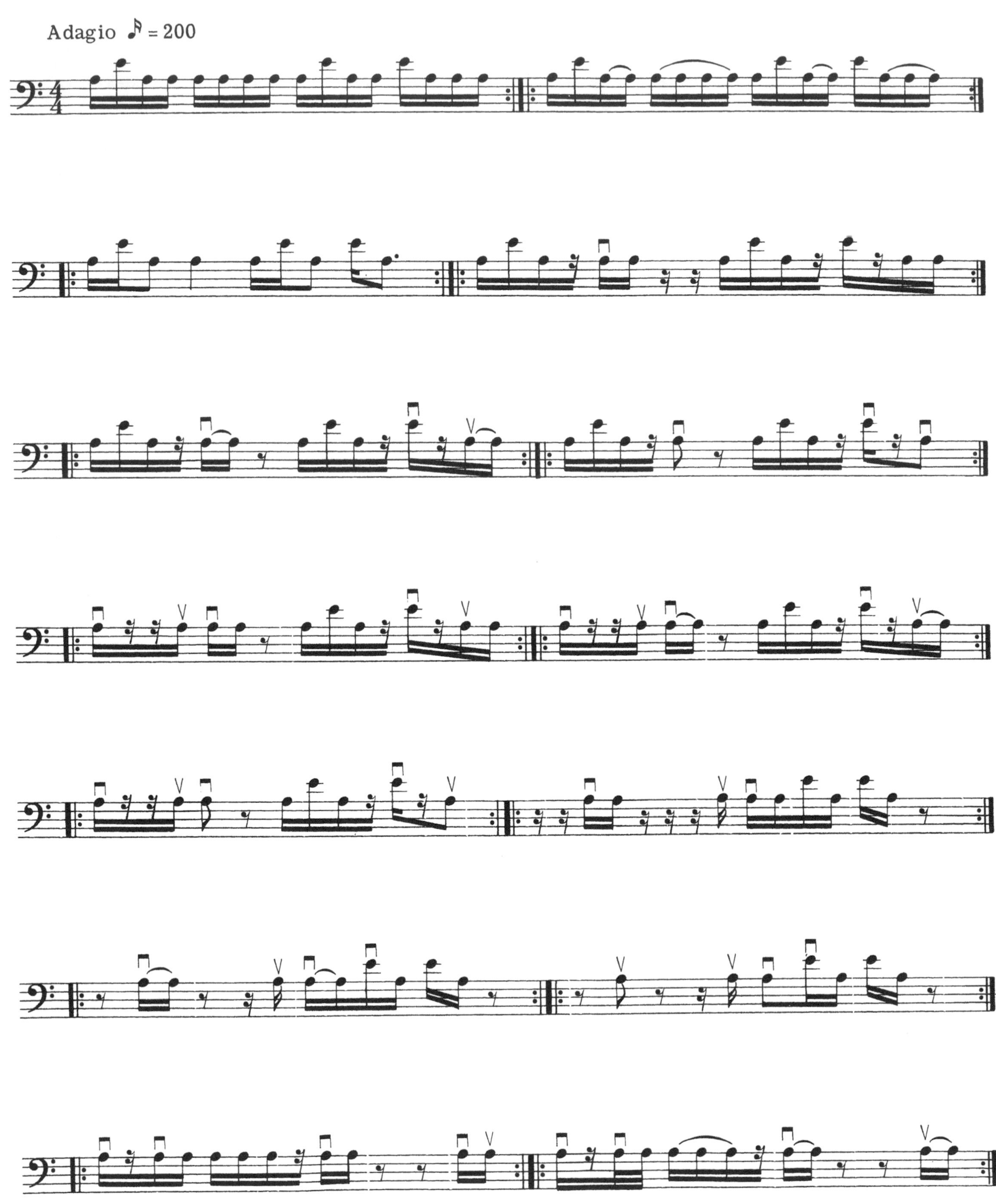
Adagio ♪ = 200

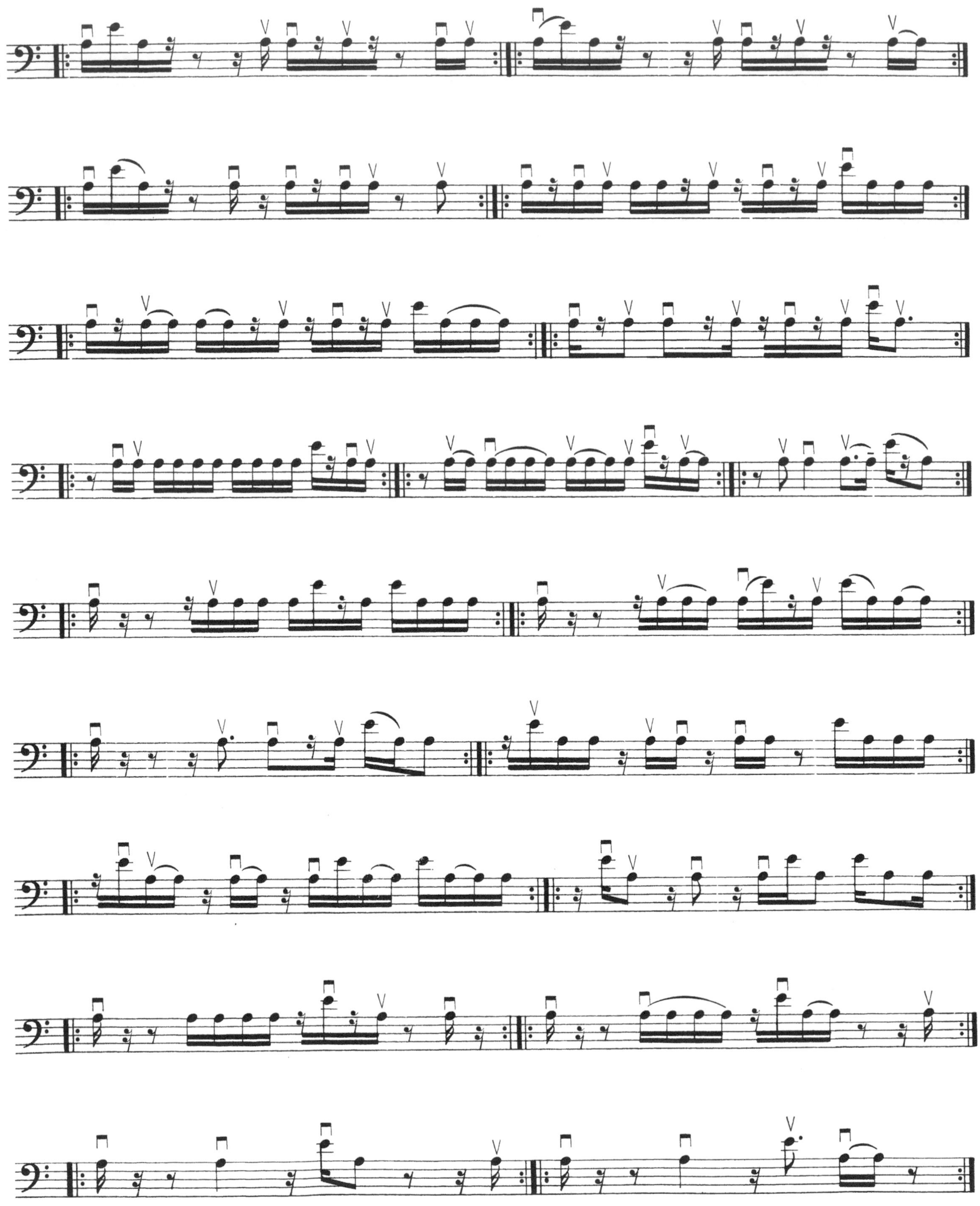